Last Minute Revision

MATHEMATICS WORKBOOK 1

Useful for Unit Tests, School Examinations & Olympiads

Author
Prasoon Kumar
Peer Reviewer
Jyotsna Gopikrishnan

As per Updated CBSE Pattern

Strictly According to Latest NCERT Syllabus

Published by:

F-2/16, Ansari road, Daryaganj, New Delhi-110002
☎ 23240026, 23240027 • *Fax:* 011-23240028
Email: info@vspublishers.com • *Website:* www.vspublishers.com
Online Brandstore: amazon.in/vspublishers

Regional Office : Hyderabad
5-1-707/1, Brij Bhawan (Beside Central Bank of India Lane)
Bank Street, Koti, Hyderabad - 500 095
☎ 040-24737290
E-mail: vspublishershyd@gmail.com

Branch Office : Mumbai
Jaywant Industrial Estate, 1st Floor–108, Tardeo Road
Opposite Sobo Central Mall, Mumbai – 400 034
☎ 022-23510736
E-mail: vspublishersmum@gmail.com

ISBN 978-93-579424-4-7
Edition 2020

DISCLAIMER

Publisher's Note

The current decade has firmly established V&S Publishers as one of the leading publishers of general trade mass appeal books across popular genres in India. With over 800 titles available in print and digital versions, we cater to readers worldwide via popular e-commerce platforms, booksellers and chain stores. We serve people from all strata of society by publishing books that are informative yet affordable. Our primary categories are Self-help, Student Development, Children, Health and Language Learning.

Keeping pace with emerging trends and market demands, we stepped into long-felt searching need to publish academic books. We, at V&S Publishers, felt that there was a need to publish student-centric books, which are presented in a unique manner. This realization led us into creating books that had content put together imaginatively yet serving the same purpose of preparing students for various exams.

Based on this ideology, our series of Olympiad titles (including a proprietary online version for Olympiad test preparation) from class 1 to 10 in the subjects of Science, Mathematics, Computers and English have revolutionized the way books are written and have rightfully received outstanding response from students and parents alike. The sale of each title, as reported by booksellers, remains the high watermark in annals of Olympiad examination preparatory books.

Encouraged further by the wide acceptability of our Olympiad series, we decided to enlarge our sphere of activity by publishing Workbooks – developed to help students become exam-ready. The books currently being published are on the subjects Science, Mathematics, Computer, Social Science, English, Hindi and General Knowledge. You can treat this book as a part of Last Minute Revision series, which has been written keeping in mind how students actually prepare for various exams. The students, in order to score high, resort to unethical methods like cramming & cheating besides undergoing stressful eye-burning studies, which often leads to them faltering in the exam. This series of books is our way of helping students do a last-minute revision just before the exam.

Unlike other run-of-the-mill published Workbooks that are just about stereotypes replicating the Long answer, Short answer, Multiple choice questions etc. from a chosen chapter and surreptitiously selling as guide books, our series covers the same chapter but in a holistically wider manner. These Workbooks are written as per NCERT syllabi and comprises key concepts and MCQs and have been prepared with updated syllabus-precision so that any student who ticks (darkens the circle) 80-90% correct answers in the OMR sheet can expect to do well in the exams. Note that important concepts in point-wise format have also been summarised in the beginning of the chapter for ease in revision. This will help the student not only to discuss the subject across the class confidently, but also to score high in all Unit tests, school exams and Semester papers. Moreover, going through a workbook immediately prior to exam will just be a matter of few hours. We are positive that this novel initiative by V&S Publishers' editorial team will help students prepare well without any stress.

We wish you the best!

P.S. If you come across any error, howsoever minor, anywhere in the book, do not hesitate to discuss with your teachers while pointing that out to us in no uncertain terms. V&S Publishers does not advocate the idea of end-moment studies and advises students to prepare and study on a daily basis. These books are written with a clear objective of final revisions only.

Contents

WORKBOOK

1 Number Sense

- A number is an idea, where the symbols used to represent the numbers are called numbers.
- The digits 0, 1, 2, 3, 4, 5, 6, 7, 8 and 9 are used to form numbers or numerals.
- The numbers 1, 2, 3, ……used for counting things are called counting numbers.

1 – One	11 – Eleven
2 – Two	12 – Twelve
3 – Three	13 – Thirteen
4 – Four	14 – Fourteen
5 – Five	15 – Fifteen
6 – Six	16 – Sixteen
7 – Seven	17 – Seventeen
8 – Eight	18 – Eighteen
9 – Nine	19 – Nineteen
10 – Ten	20 – Twenty

- Zero does not have any value on its own, but acts as a place holder.
- A three digit number can be written in hundreds, tens and ones. Example, 200 – 2 hundreds 0 tens and 0 ones.
- For forming the greatest 2 digit number, place the bigger digit at tens place and the smaller digit at ones place.
- Numbers such as 1st, 2nd, 3rd, 4th, 5th, 6th, 7th, 8th, 9th, and 10th specify the position of an object in an ordered collection. These numbers are called ordinal numbers.
- Smallest two-digit number is 1 more than largest one digit number i.e. 10 is 1 more than 9.
- 99 is the greatest two digit number
- 10 is the smallest two digit number
- 100 is the smallest three digit number.

Multiple Choice Questions

1. The greatest one-digit number is 9. What is its number name?
   (a) Ten (b) Nine
   (c) Five (d) Two
2. When one is added to the greatest four-digit number, what is the result?
   (a) Smallest 4-digit number
   (b) Smallest 5-digt number
   (c) Greatest 5-digit number
   (d) Greatest 4-digit number
3. Make the greatest four digit number by using any digit twice from 3, 8, 7?
   (a) 8378 (b) 8873
   (c) 3387 (d) 7783
4. Which pair has same digits at hundreds place?
   (a) 4232, 4341 (b) 5432, 6922
   (c) 6524, 7823 (d) 2334, 2340
5. Arrange the numbers in ascending order 7, 2, 3, 8.
   (a) 2, 3, 7, 8 (b) 3, 2, 8, 7
   (c) 8, 7, 3, 2 (d) 3, 8, 2, 7
6. Which number is between 48 and 50?
   (a) 47 (b) 49
   (c) 51 (d) 52
7. What comes after 35?
   (a) 34 (b) 37
   (c) 36 (d) 38
8. What comes before 76?
   (a) 73 (b) 74
   (c) 77 (d) 75
9. What comes before 89?
   (a) Eighty-eight (b) Ninety
   (c) Ninety-one (d) Eighty-seven
10. The decimal number system contains_______ digits.
    (a) 9 (b) 10
    (c) 8 (d) 100
11. _______ has no predecessor.
    (a) zero (b) one
    (c) ten (d) 100
12. Order these numbers from lowest to highest.
    12, 25, 18, 23, 14
    (a) 23, 14, 18, 25, 12
    (b) 25, 23, 18, 14, 12
    (c) 12, 14, 18, 23, 25
    (d) 14, 12, 18, 23, 25
13. 232, 242 _____ 262. The missing number in the pattern is _______.
    (a) 222 (b) 252
    (c) 253 (d) 243
14. Between which two numbers is 66?
    (a) 65 and 67 (b) 63 and 65
    (c) 64 and 65 (d) 65 and 68
15. Which number comes after ninety-nine?
    (a) 100 (b) 98
    (c) 96 (d) 97
16. How many tens are in fifty-two?
    (a) 2 (b) 5
    (c) 7 (d) 6
17. What comes after 92?
    (a) Ninety-three (b) Ninety-four
    (c) Ninety (d) Ninety-one
18. What is the ordinal number of 9?
    (a) Sixth (b) Ninth
    (c) Seventh (d) Eight
19. What is the number name of the smallest one-digit number?
    (a) five (b) one
    (c) three (d) two
20. What is the number name of greatest one-digit number?
    (a) Five (b) Eight
    (c) Six (d) Nine

21. What is the number name of the smallest two-digit number?
(a) Ten (b) Nine
(c) Twelve (d) Eleven

22. What is the number name of the greatest two digit number?
(a) Ninety – five (b) Ninety – nine
(c) Ninety – four (d) Ninety – six

23. Choose the one that is wrong.
(a) Four-5 (b) Seven-7
(c) Zero-0 (d) Nine-9

24. How many tens are there in 352?
(a) 5 (b) 35
(c) 52 (d) 523

25. The number 932 has ______ hundreds.
(a) 9 (b) 3
(c) 4 (d) 2

26. The greatest three digit number among the following is ______.
(a) 256 (b) 252
(c) 168 (d) 356

27. The greatest three digit odd number is ______.
(a) 303 (b) 039
(c) 309 (d) 305

28. The smallest 3-digit number is ________.
(a) 100 (b) 101
(c) 102 (d) 120

29. Which of the following numbers has 6 in hundred place?
(a) 963 (b) 693
(c) 396 (d) 936

30. Between which two numbers is 73?
(a) 70 and 71 (b) 74 and 75
(c) 72 and 74 (d) 71 and 72

31. Order these numbers from lowest to highest and choose the correct option.
17, 25, 30, 24, 21, 18
(a) 21, 25, 24, 17, 18, 30
(b) 18, 17, 24, 25, 30, 21
(c) 17, 18, 24, 25, 21, 30
(d) 17, 18, 21, 24, 25, 30

32. How many chillies are there in this figure? 
(a) 10 (b) 15
(c) 17 (d) 16

33. Which of the following has 5 objects?
(a)
(b) 
(c) 
(d)

34. Which of the following has the number name 4?
(a) 
(b) 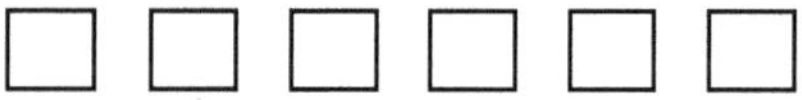
(c) 
(d)

35. How many insects are there in this figure?  
(a) 3 (b) 2 
(c) 4 (d) 6

36. How many oxes are there in this figure?

(a) 2 (b) 1
(c) 3 (d) 5

37. Which number comes after 102?
(a) One-hundred two
(b) One hundred three
(c) One hundred six
(d) One hundred five

38. What comes before 45 ?
(a) forty-six
(b) forty-two
(c) forty-four
(d) forty-eight

39. What comes before 101?
(a) Hundred
(b) One hundred two
(c) One hundred three
(d) One hundred six

40. Between which two numbers is 107?
(a) 105 & 108 (b) 108 & 111
(c) 105 & 107 (d) 106 & 108

41. What will come in place of the question mark?

(a) 74 (b) 78 (c) 76 (d) 73

42. The given number line shows which of the following.

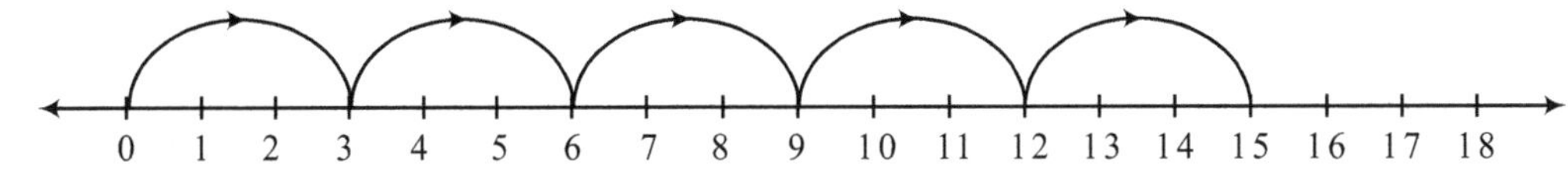

(a) Counting by 2's (b) Counting by 3's (c) Counting by 4's (d) Counting by 1's

43. Which of the following is not a correct match?

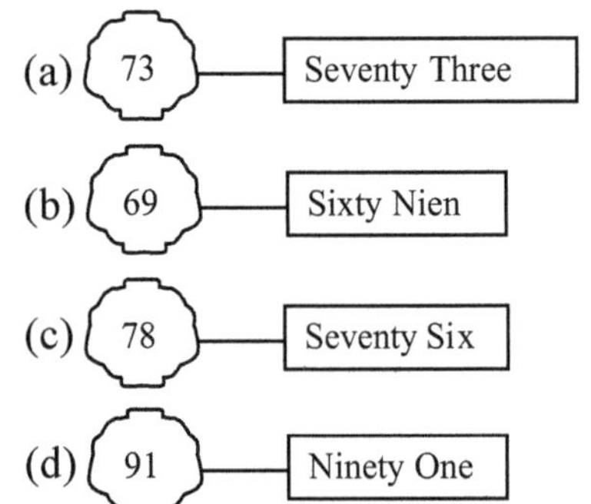

44. Which of the following holds largest number?

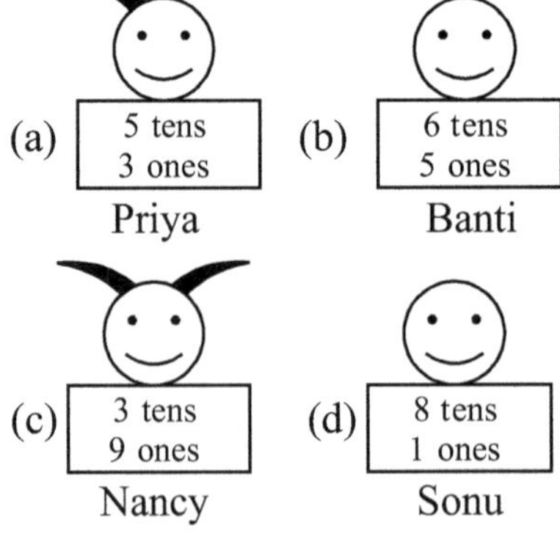

45. What is the ascending order of 39, 52, 17, 29, 76?
(a) 29, 17, 39, 52, 76
(b) 52, 76, 39, 17, 29
(c) 76, 52, 39, 39, 17
(d) 17, 29, 39, 52, 76

46. Which of the following jars has least number of balls?

(a) 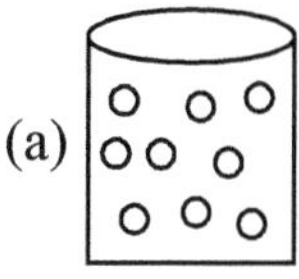

(b) 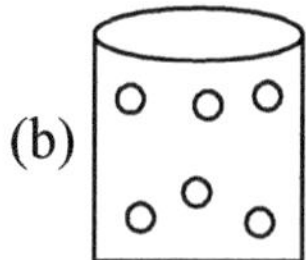

(c) 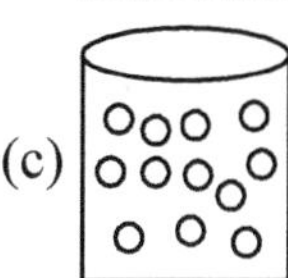

(d) 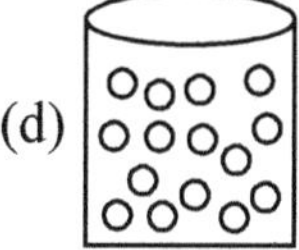

47. How many rats are there in given picture?

(a) 8
(b) 10
(c) 11
(d) 12

48. Which bowl has maximum number of apples?

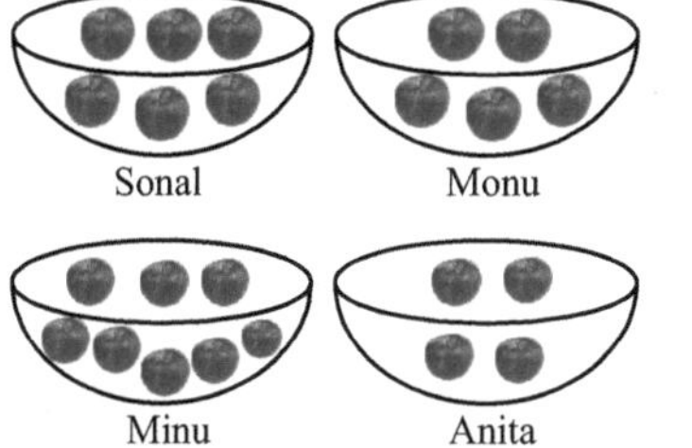

(a) Sonal
(b) Anita
(c) Minu
(d) Monu

49. Five rats are numbered as follows:

Which rat shows the number lying between 60 and 70 and has 8 at ones place?

(a) 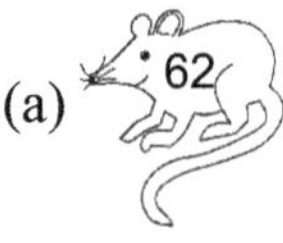

(b) 

(c) 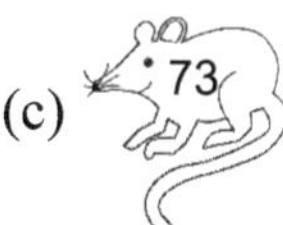

(d) 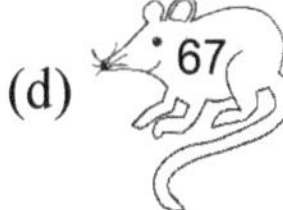

50. Which of the following sets has more objects than the given set of dots?

(a) 

(b)

(c)

(d)

51. The given number line shows ....

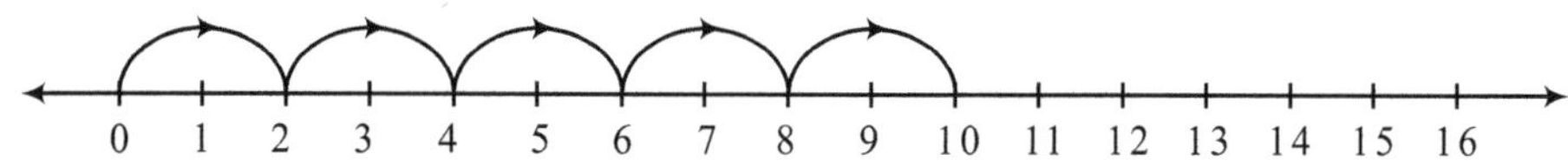

(a) Counting by 1's (b) Counting by 2's (c) Counting by 3's (d) Counting by 4's

52. The number on the given abacus is ______.

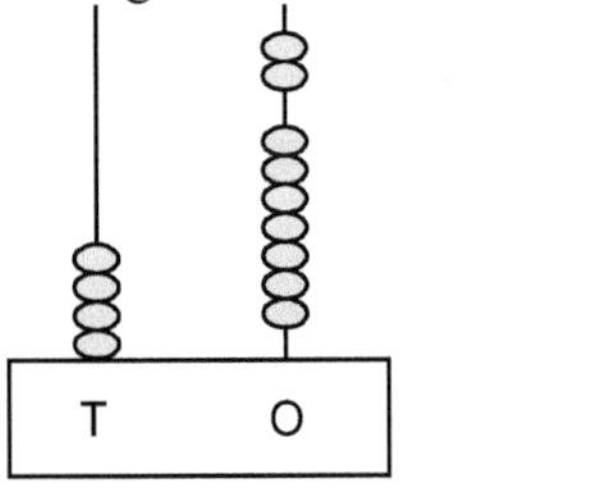

(a) 49 (b) 39

(c) 48 (d) 47

53. What comes before 90 and after 88?

(a) 87 (b) 86

(c) 89 (d) 91

54. Which of the following is in descending order?

(a) 48, 45, 61, 57 (b) 45, 48, 57, 61

(c) 61, 57, 48, 45 (d) 61, 48, 57, 45

55. Which of the following comes after 58 and before 60?

(a) 57 (b) 59 (c) 61 (d) 56

56. Which of the following is a correct match?

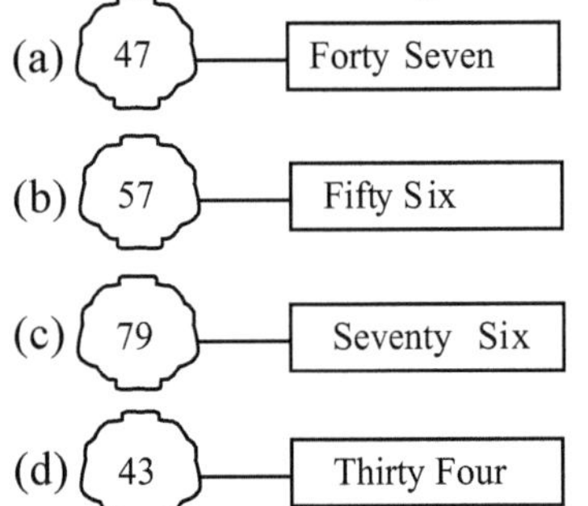

57. Which of the following has smallest number?

(a) Manju (b) Raju

(c) Manoj (d) Rani

58. Which abacus shows 1 more than 43?

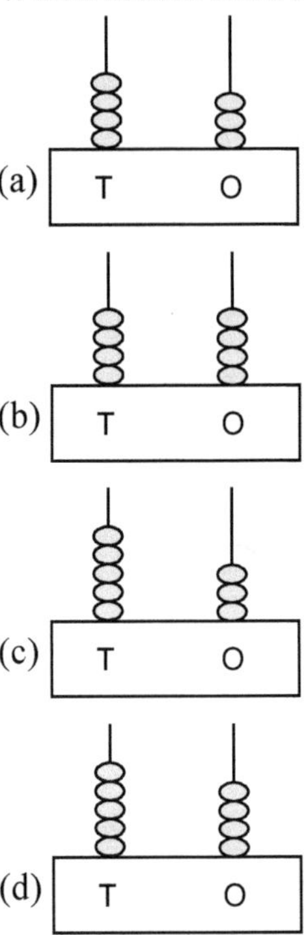

59. Which number line shows counting by 2's?

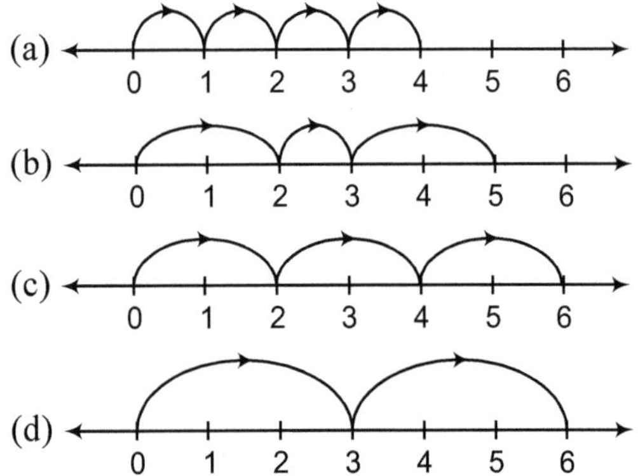

60. Which of the following is less than 67 and greater than 65?

(a) 66 (b) 64

(c) 68 (d) 69

Darken Your Choice with HB Pencil

1.	ⓐ	ⓑ	ⓒ	ⓓ	13.	ⓐ	ⓑ	ⓒ	ⓓ	25.	ⓐ	ⓑ	ⓒ	ⓓ	37.	ⓐ	ⓑ	ⓒ	ⓓ	49.	ⓐ	ⓑ	ⓒ	ⓓ
2.	ⓐ	ⓑ	ⓒ	ⓓ	14.	ⓐ	ⓑ	ⓒ	ⓓ	26.	ⓐ	ⓑ	ⓒ	ⓓ	38.	ⓐ	ⓑ	ⓒ	ⓓ	50.	ⓐ	ⓑ	ⓒ	ⓓ
3.	ⓐ	ⓑ	ⓒ	ⓓ	15.	ⓐ	ⓑ	ⓒ	ⓓ	27.	ⓐ	ⓑ	ⓒ	ⓓ	39.	ⓐ	ⓑ	ⓒ	ⓓ	51.	ⓐ	ⓑ	ⓒ	ⓓ
4.	ⓐ	ⓑ	ⓒ	ⓓ	16.	ⓐ	ⓑ	ⓒ	ⓓ	28.	ⓐ	ⓑ	ⓒ	ⓓ	40.	ⓐ	ⓑ	ⓒ	ⓓ	52.	ⓐ	ⓑ	ⓒ	ⓓ
5.	ⓐ	ⓑ	ⓒ	ⓓ	17.	ⓐ	ⓑ	ⓒ	ⓓ	29.	ⓐ	ⓑ	ⓒ	ⓓ	41.	ⓐ	ⓑ	ⓒ	ⓓ	53.	ⓐ	ⓑ	ⓒ	ⓓ
6.	ⓐ	ⓑ	ⓒ	ⓓ	18.	ⓐ	ⓑ	ⓒ	ⓓ	30.	ⓐ	ⓑ	ⓒ	ⓓ	42.	ⓐ	ⓑ	ⓒ	ⓓ	54.	ⓐ	ⓑ	ⓒ	ⓓ
7.	ⓐ	ⓑ	ⓒ	ⓓ	19.	ⓐ	ⓑ	ⓒ	ⓓ	31.	ⓐ	ⓑ	ⓒ	ⓓ	43.	ⓐ	ⓑ	ⓒ	ⓓ	55.	ⓐ	ⓑ	ⓒ	ⓓ
8.	ⓐ	ⓑ	ⓒ	ⓓ	20.	ⓐ	ⓑ	ⓒ	ⓓ	32.	ⓐ	ⓑ	ⓒ	ⓓ	44.	ⓐ	ⓑ	ⓒ	ⓓ	56.	ⓐ	ⓑ	ⓒ	ⓓ
9.	ⓐ	ⓑ	ⓒ	ⓓ	21.	ⓐ	ⓑ	ⓒ	ⓓ	33.	ⓐ	ⓑ	ⓒ	ⓓ	45.	ⓐ	ⓑ	ⓒ	ⓓ	57.	ⓐ	ⓑ	ⓒ	ⓓ
10.	ⓐ	ⓑ	ⓒ	ⓓ	22.	ⓐ	ⓑ	ⓒ	ⓓ	34.	ⓐ	ⓑ	ⓒ	ⓓ	46.	ⓐ	ⓑ	ⓒ	ⓓ	58.	ⓐ	ⓑ	ⓒ	ⓓ
11.	ⓐ	ⓑ	ⓒ	ⓓ	23.	ⓐ	ⓑ	ⓒ	ⓓ	35.	ⓐ	ⓑ	ⓒ	ⓓ	47.	ⓐ	ⓑ	ⓒ	ⓓ	59.	ⓐ	ⓑ	ⓒ	ⓓ
12.	ⓐ	ⓑ	ⓒ	ⓓ	24.	ⓐ	ⓑ	ⓒ	ⓓ	36.	ⓐ	ⓑ	ⓒ	ⓓ	48.	ⓐ	ⓑ	ⓒ	ⓓ	60.	ⓐ	ⓑ	ⓒ	ⓓ

WORKBOOK

2 Addition

- Counting things together is called addition. It is denoted by the sign (+) called plus.
- The numbers that are added are called addends and the answer we get on adding is called sum.

  Example : $9 + 3 = 12$, $4 + 3 = 7$
- A line with number at equal places on it is called a number line.

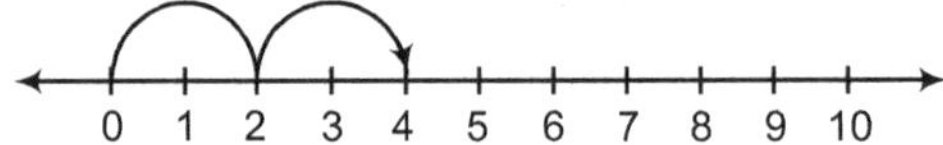

- The sum of three numbers is the same even if we change the grouping of the numbers.
- Adding 0 to any number gives the same number as the sum.

  Example : $4 + 0 = 4$, $0 + 8 = 8$,

  $0 + 10 = 10$, $13 + 0 = 13$.
- Add the ones first, then the tens and finally the hundreds.

H	T	O
2	4	3
6	2	4
8	6	7

- If we change the order of numbers, the sum remains the same (*i.e.*, $5 + 4 = 4 + 5$)
- The result of adding two or more numbers

  Example : $1 + 3 + 6 = 10$
- The addition of two whole numbers is the total amount of those quantities combined.
- While adding, if we change the order of the given numbers, the result will be the same.

Multiple Choice Questions

1. Which of the following is incorrect sum?
   (a) 5 + 3 = 8 (b) 4 + 4 = 8
   (c) 5 + 5 = 10 (d) 5 + 4 = 8
2. I have 8 apples. Raju gave me 8 more. Ravi gave me 3 more. How many apples I have?
   (a) 11 (b) 19
   (c) 21 (d) 29
3. There are 20 boys and 15 girls in a class. How many children are there in the class?
   (a) 35 (b) 45
   (c) 40 (d) 42
4. Raju has 16 balls and Priya has 20 balls. Total number of balls is equal to ________.
   (a) 20 (b) 26
   (c) 36 (d) 25
5. Which of the following is correct sum?
   (a) 8 + 2 = 11 (b) 2 + 6 = 9
   (c) 7 + 2 = 11 (d) 9 + 2 = 11
6. Find the missing number ________ + 3 = 7
   (a) 4 (b) 2
   (c) 1 (d) 3
7. The weight of a cow is 125 kg. The buffalo's weight is 10 kg more than the cow's weight. What is the weight of the buffalo?
   (a) 135 kg (b) 185 kg
   (c) 125 kg (d) 145 kg
8. What should be added to 5 to obtain 11?
   (a) 3 (b) 6
   (c) 5 (d) 7
9. There are 30 apples in a bowl. Ravi puts 40 apples into it from his bag. How many apples are there in the bowl altogether?
   (a) 48 (b) 78
   (c) 70 (d) 80
10. Choose the correct addition fact for the given figure.

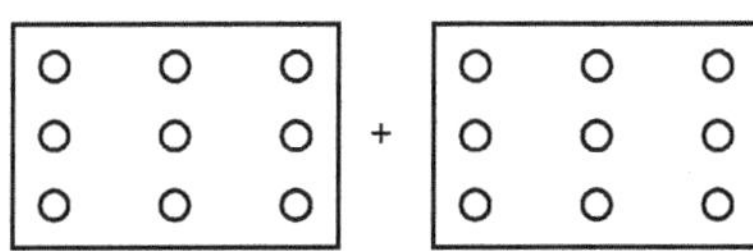

   (a) 16 (b) 15
   (c) 11 (d) 18

11. A boy jumps 2 steps from 0 and then 3 steps. Where will he reach?
   (a) 5th point (b) 6th point
   (c) 7th point (d) 4th point
12. Number of balls in all three boxes is equal to ______.

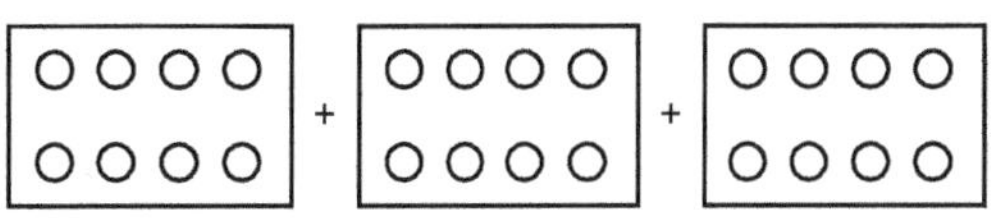

   (a) 17 (b) 15
   (c) 27 (d) 24
13. One number for 800 + 9000 + 1 is equal to ______.
   (a) 8901 (b) 8091
   (c) 9801 (d) 8019
14. Which adds up to 12?
   (a) 6 + 6 (b) 5 + 7
   (c) 10 + 2 (d) All of these
15. How much is 5 tens and 3 ones?
   (a) 503 (b) 53
   (c) 5300 (d) 530
16. _____ comes just before 320
   (a) 319 (b) 317
   (c) 321 (d) 318
17. 10 + 37 + 43 = ________
   (a) 77 (b) 90
   (c) 67 (d) 197
18. What is the missing number?_____ + 10 = 17
   (a) 17 (b) 1
   (c) 7 (d) 16
19. Fill the missing number 5 + _____ = 15
   (a) 8 (b) 10
   (c) 12 (d) 5
20. What is the answer? 16 + 12 = _____.
   (a) 29 (b) 30
   (c) 28 (d) 32
21. I have 8 biscuits. Ravi gave me 4 more. Aman gave me 4 more. How many biscuits I have?
   (a) 12 (b) 15
   (c) 14 (d) 16

22. Sita got 40 marks in science and 54 marks in maths. How much marks did she get in all?
(a) 96 (b) 90
(c) 94 (d) 80

23. Gita bought 10 pencils on Monday, 20 pencils on Tuesday and 25 pencils on Wednesday. How many pencils did she buy altogether?
(a) 35 (b) 55
(c) 45 (d) 65

24. Which is more?
(a) 14 + 3 (b) 21 + 7
(c) 22 + 7 (d) 19 + 6

25. Which adds up to 18?
(a) 16 + 2 (b) 15 + 3
(c) 9 + 9 (d) All of these

26. Find the missing number __ + 6 = 18
(a) 12 (b) 11
(c) 13 (d) 14

27. After spending ₹ 40, Aman had ₹ 200 left. How much did he have at first?
(a) 240 (b) 200
(c) 204 (d) 160

28. The next number in the series.
16, 20, 24, 28, 32 is ______.
(a) 30 (b) 34
(c) 38 (d) 36

29. We add smallest one-digit number and greatest one-digit number to get?
(a) Six (b) Ten
(c) Eleven (d) Eight

30. 6 tens + 8 is equal to ______.
(a) 62 (b) 72
(c) 68 (d) 78

31. + = ______ strawberries.
(a) 4 (b) 6
(c) 5 (d) 9

32. There are 18 apples in a basket. Ravi puts 9 more apples in it. How many apples are there in the basket now?
(a) 9 (b) 26
(c) 30 (d) 27

33. + = ______.
(a) 10 (b) 7
(c) 8 (d) 9

34. Which is more?
(a) 90 + 2 (b) 107 + 6
(c) 50 + 8 (d) 10 + 210

35. Which of the following is correct sum?
(a) 16 + 8 = 24 (b) 12 + 2 = 13
(c) 15 + 5 = 21 (d) 13 + 4 = 18

36. Priya has 30 balls. She buys another 15 balls. How many balls does she have altogether?
(a) 25 (b) 35
(c) 30 (d) 45

37. There are 50 boys and 10 girls in a class. How many children are there in the class?
(a) 70 (b) 50
(c) 60 (d) 40

38. The age of Rohit is 20 years and the age of Rahul is 10 year more than Rohit's age. What is the age of Rahul?
(a) 10 years (b) 25 years
(c) 30 years (d) 27 years

39. 2 tens ? ones + 4 tens 6 ones = 81
(a) 52 (b) 15
(c) 33 (d) 107

40. After spending ₹ 100, Hari had ₹ 10 left. How did he have at first?
(a) ₹ 110 (b) ₹ 90
(c) ₹ 80 (d) ₹ 120

41. If I add a number to 50, I will get 50. What number am I adding?

50 + □ = 50

(a) 0 (b) 1
(c) 10 (d) 2

42. Find the missing number 18 + ☐ = 27

(a) 7 (b) 8

(c) 9 (d) 6

43. Which of the following options gives the number greater than 47?

(a) 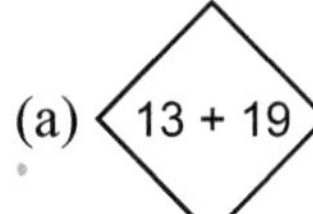

(b) 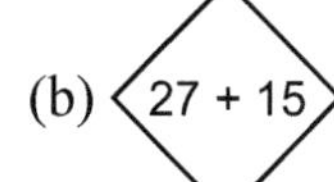

(c) 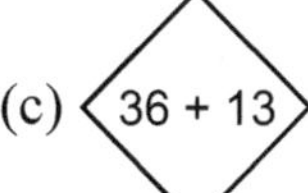

(d) 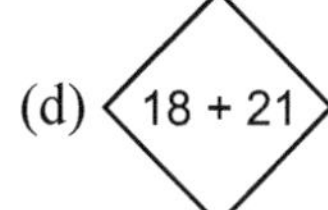

44. Which of the following options gives the answer as 59?

(a) 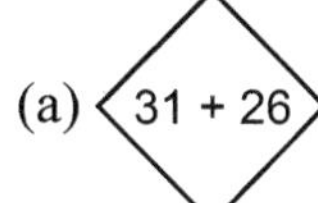

(b) 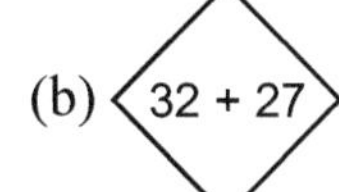

(c) 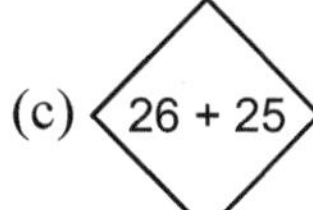

(d) 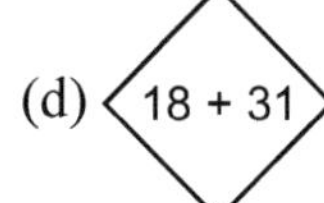

45. There are only 9 parrots, 8 pigeons, 8 hens and 5 chicks in a farm. How many birds are there in the farm?

(a) 28 (b) 30

(c) 31 (d) 29

46. Sonali bought 17 toys on Sunday, 9 toys on Monday and 12 toys on Tuesday. How many toys did she buy altogether?

(a) 38 (b) 36

(c) 39 (d) 42

47. Monu has 46 chocolates. He buys 7 more chocolates. How many chocolates does he have altogether?

(a) 60 (b) 57

(c) 53 (d) 54

48. Which of the following is incorrect match?

(a) (37) + (42) = 79

(b) (46) + (23) = 69

(c) (58) + (31) = 88

(d) (35) + (42) = 77

49. Which of the following options has smallest value?

(a) 52 + 7 (b) 51 + 3

(c) 51 + 8 (d) 62 + 7

50. Which of the following options has largest value?

(a) 72 + 4 (b) 83 + 5

(c) 64 + 3 (d) 82 + 3

51. Arrange the rats from largest to smallest?

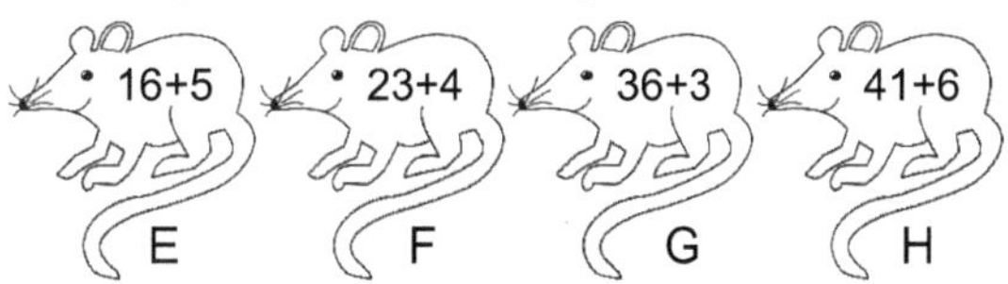

(a) H, G, F, E (b) G, H, E, F

(c) E, F, G, H (d) H, E, F, G

52. Number of pictures in both the boxes is _____.

Box M

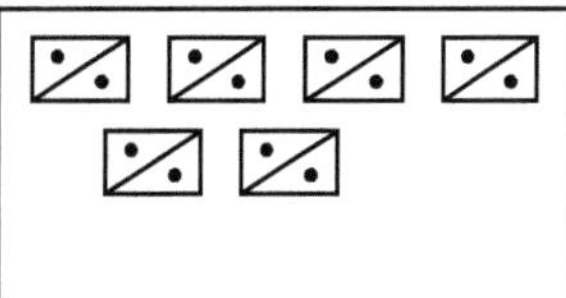

Box N

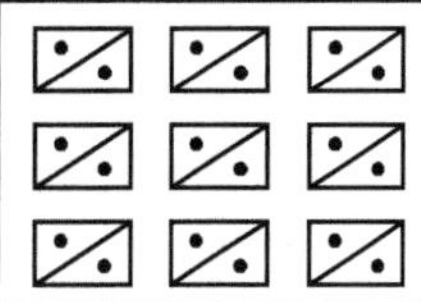

(a) 5 + 8 (b) 6 + 9

(c) 5 + 9 (d) 6 + 8

53. 12 + 4 is shown by which abacus?

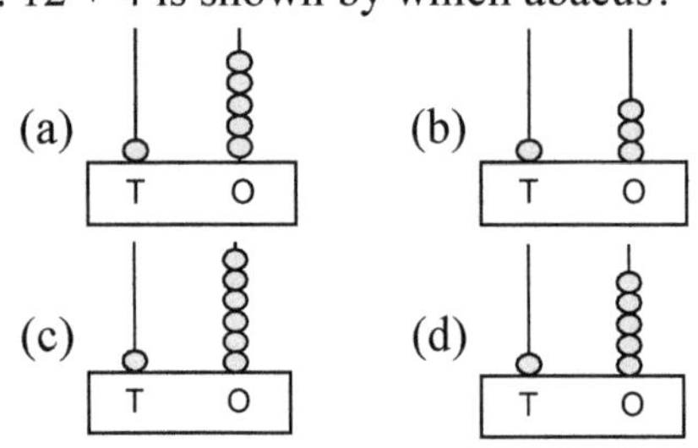

54. Which of the following options will complete the given number bond?

(a) 20 ones + 5 tens (b) 6 tens + 7 ones

(c) 4 tens + 3 tens (d) 7 tens + 6 ones

55. Which of the following options shows sum of the abacuses?

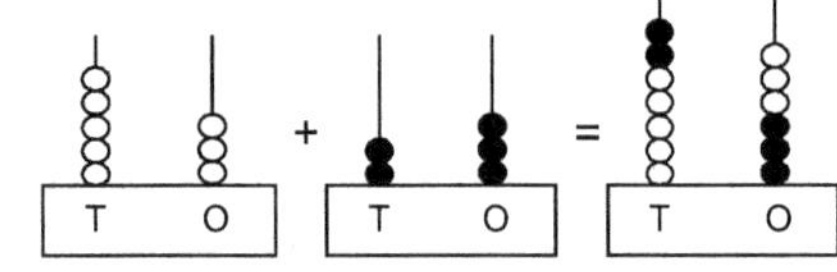

(a) 53 + 24 = 77 (b) 53 + 23 = 76

(c) 54 + 22 = 76 (d) 55 + 21 = 76

Direction (56-58): Study the given sets and answer the following questions.

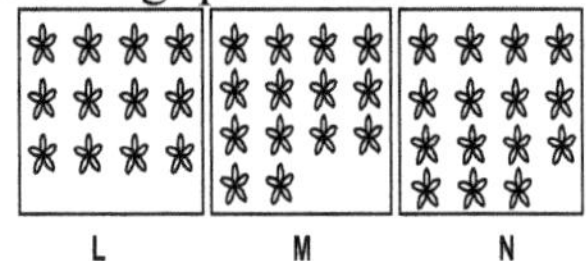

56. Find the total number of flowers in set M and N?

(a) 29 (b) 27

(c) 30 (d) 31

57. Find the total number of flowers in sets L and N?

(a) 21 (b) 23

(c) 27 (d) 25

58. Find the total number of flowers in all the given sets?

(a) 38 (b) 39

(c) 40 (d) 41

59. Which of the following options gives the answer less than 39?

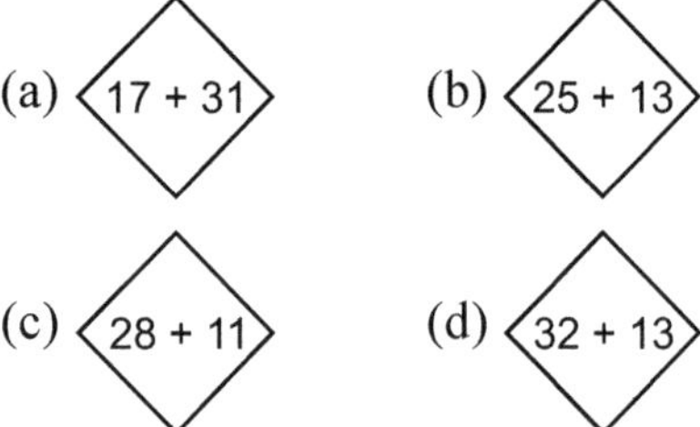

60. In a garden, there are 15 cows, 11 goats and 22 sheeps. How many animals are there in the garden?

(a) 46 (b) 47

(c) 48 (d) 49

Darken Your Choice with HB Pencil

1.	ⓐ	ⓑ	ⓒ	ⓓ	13.	ⓐ	ⓑ	ⓒ	ⓓ	25.	ⓐ	ⓑ	ⓒ	ⓓ	37.	ⓐ	ⓑ	ⓒ	ⓓ	49.	ⓐ	ⓑ	ⓒ	ⓓ
2.	ⓐ	ⓑ	ⓒ	ⓓ	14.	ⓐ	ⓑ	ⓒ	ⓓ	26.	ⓐ	ⓑ	ⓒ	ⓓ	38.	ⓐ	ⓑ	ⓒ	ⓓ	50.	ⓐ	ⓑ	ⓒ	ⓓ
3.	ⓐ	ⓑ	ⓒ	ⓓ	15.	ⓐ	ⓑ	ⓒ	ⓓ	27.	ⓐ	ⓑ	ⓒ	ⓓ	39.	ⓐ	ⓑ	ⓒ	ⓓ	51.	ⓐ	ⓑ	ⓒ	ⓓ
4.	ⓐ	ⓑ	ⓒ	ⓓ	16.	ⓐ	ⓑ	ⓒ	ⓓ	28.	ⓐ	ⓑ	ⓒ	ⓓ	40.	ⓐ	ⓑ	ⓒ	ⓓ	52.	ⓐ	ⓑ	ⓒ	ⓓ
5.	ⓐ	ⓑ	ⓒ	ⓓ	17.	ⓐ	ⓑ	ⓒ	ⓓ	29.	ⓐ	ⓑ	ⓒ	ⓓ	41.	ⓐ	ⓑ	ⓒ	ⓓ	53.	ⓐ	ⓑ	ⓒ	ⓓ
6.	ⓐ	ⓑ	ⓒ	ⓓ	18.	ⓐ	ⓑ	ⓒ	ⓓ	30.	ⓐ	ⓑ	ⓒ	ⓓ	42.	ⓐ	ⓑ	ⓒ	ⓓ	54.	ⓐ	ⓑ	ⓒ	ⓓ
7.	ⓐ	ⓑ	ⓒ	ⓓ	19.	ⓐ	ⓑ	ⓒ	ⓓ	31.	ⓐ	ⓑ	ⓒ	ⓓ	43.	ⓐ	ⓑ	ⓒ	ⓓ	55.	ⓐ	ⓑ	ⓒ	ⓓ
8.	ⓐ	ⓑ	ⓒ	ⓓ	20.	ⓐ	ⓑ	ⓒ	ⓓ	32.	ⓐ	ⓑ	ⓒ	ⓓ	44.	ⓐ	ⓑ	ⓒ	ⓓ	56.	ⓐ	ⓑ	ⓒ	ⓓ
9.	ⓐ	ⓑ	ⓒ	ⓓ	21.	ⓐ	ⓑ	ⓒ	ⓓ	33.	ⓐ	ⓑ	ⓒ	ⓓ	45.	ⓐ	ⓑ	ⓒ	ⓓ	57.	ⓐ	ⓑ	ⓒ	ⓓ
10.	ⓐ	ⓑ	ⓒ	ⓓ	22.	ⓐ	ⓑ	ⓒ	ⓓ	34.	ⓐ	ⓑ	ⓒ	ⓓ	46.	ⓐ	ⓑ	ⓒ	ⓓ	58.	ⓐ	ⓑ	ⓒ	ⓓ
11.	ⓐ	ⓑ	ⓒ	ⓓ	23.	ⓐ	ⓑ	ⓒ	ⓓ	35.	ⓐ	ⓑ	ⓒ	ⓓ	47.	ⓐ	ⓑ	ⓒ	ⓓ	59.	ⓐ	ⓑ	ⓒ	ⓓ
12.	ⓐ	ⓑ	ⓒ	ⓓ	24.	ⓐ	ⓑ	ⓒ	ⓓ	36.	ⓐ	ⓑ	ⓒ	ⓓ	48.	ⓐ	ⓑ	ⓒ	ⓓ	60.	ⓐ	ⓑ	ⓒ	ⓓ

WORKBOOK

3 Subtraction

- Subtraction is the opposite of addition. The symbol for subtraction is (–) and is read as minus.
- The number from which another number is taken away is called minuend.
- The number that is taken away is called subtrahend.
- The answer we get by subtracting a given number from other is called difference.
  Example : 10 – 2 = 8, 6 – 4 = 2
- Subtracting 0 from a number gives the number itself as difference. Example : 4 – 0 = 4

  [○○ ○○] – [ ] = [○○ ○○]

- Subtracting a number from the number itself gives 0 as difference. Example: 6 – 6 = 0

  [○○○ ○○○] – [○○○ ○○○] = [ ]

- Subtract 9 from 45.

```
 T O
 4 5
 – 9
 ---
 3 6
```

- Zero subtracted from any number is equal to the number itself.
- First we subtract ones then tens and then hundreds.
- Subtract 352 from 700

```
  H T O
  7 0 0
– 3 5 2
  -----
  3 4 8
```

Multiple Choice Questions

1. Ravi had 70 marbles. He gave Kiran 20 marbles. How many marbles are left with Ravi?
   (a) 40 (b) 90
   (c) 60 (d) 50
2. My book has 28 pages. I've read 23 pages. How many pages are left to read?
   (a) 6 (b) 2
   (c) 4 (d) 5
3. Fill in the missing number 6 – ……= 5
   (a) 0 (b) 1
   (c) 2 (d) 3
4. How is 14 less than 40 written?
   (a) 21 (b) 16
   (c) 26 (d) 29
5. Which of the following gives the greatest even number as the answer?
   (a) 20 – 6 (b) 30 – 21
   (c) 30 – 19 (d) 40 – 8
6. There are 10 fishes in a pond. 4 jumped off. How many are left?
   (a) 5 (b) 6
   (c) 2 (d) 8
7. A shopkeeper had 30 chocolates on Monday. He had 10 chocolates less on Wednesday. How many chocolates were sold by Wednesday?
   (a) 30 – 5 = 25 (b) 30 + 10 = 40
   (c) 30 + 15 = 45 (d) 30 – 10 = 20
8. Priya has 100 apples. She gave 45 of them to her sister Supriya. How many apples does Priya have?
   (a) 45 (b) 55
   (c) 35 (d) 65
9. Which number comes in the place of A?
   A – 19 = 40
   (a) 21 (b) 39
   (c) 49 (d) 59
10. Ragini eats 10 mangoes from a packet of 15 mangoes. How many are left?
    (a) 7 (b) 5
    (c) 8 (d) 6
11. 5 tens – 5 is equal to ________.
    (a) 40 (b) 50
    (c) 45 (d) 55
12. 2 hundred –100 is equal to ________.
    (a) 50 (b) 100
    (c) 150 (d) 200
13. What number replaces question mark to make the number sentence true?
    40 – ? = 24
    (a) 38 (b) 64
    (c) 24 (d) 16
14. 30 + 5 = ? – 3
    (a) 38 (b) 34
    (c) 37 (d) 40
15. Which of the following gives the greater odd number as the answer?
    (a) 45 – 10 (b) 45 – 12
    (c) 65 – 6 (d) 56 – 3
16. Difference between 35 and 105 is ________.
    (a) 35 (b) 65
    (c) 45 (d) 70
17. How do you make 8?
    (a) 12 – 6 (b) 18 – 10
    (c) 8 – 8 (d) 16 – 4
18. Which is not a way to make 9?
    (a) 16 – 7 (b) 12 – 2
    (c) 15 – 6 (d) 12 – 3
19. Ravi needs 14 chocolates. He already has 4 chocolates. How many more chocolates does he need?
    (a) 10 (b) 5
    (c) 8 (d) 2

20. My book has 30 Pages. I have read 25 pages. How many pages are left to read?
(a) 2 (b) 4
(c) 7 (d) 5

21. Aman's mom had 400 apples. Aman ate 50, and then gave 52 away. How many apples were left?
(a) 198 (b) 298
(c) 398 (d) None of these

22. What value of R makes this number sentence true?
60 – R = 25
(a) 35 (b) 25
(c) 45 (d) 55

23. What is the value of R?
160 – R = 60
(a) 80 (b) 120
(c) 100 (d) 110

24. Ravi had 160 pens. He lost 72 pens. How many pens does he have now?
(a) 68 (b) 78
(c) 88 (d) 98

25. I have 30 frocks. 7 are red, 8 are yellow and rest are green. How many frocks are green?
(a) 10 (b) 15
(c) 16 (d) 30

26. What is 50 less than 600?
(a) 590 (b) 540
(c) 550 (d) 450

27. A store purchased 400 eggs. 169 of eggs are yellow. How many eggs are not yellow?
(a) 200 (b) 321
(c) 213 (d) 231

28. What number is 4 less than 9999?
(a) 9969 (b) 9996
(c) 9995 (d) 9959

29. What is the difference between 529 and 129?
(a) 430 (b) 403
(c) 454 (d) 400

30. 8 tens – 5 is equal to _______.
(a) 75 (b) 72
(c) 73 (d) 81

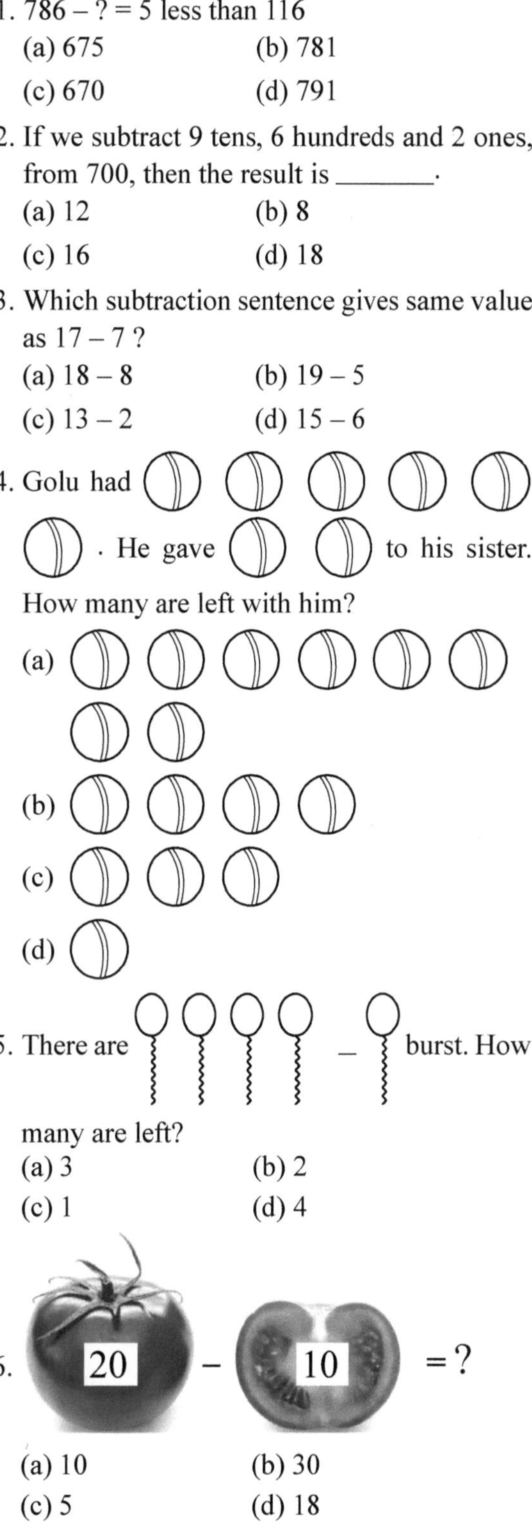

31. 786 – ? = 5 less than 116
(a) 675 (b) 781
(c) 670 (d) 791

32. If we subtract 9 tens, 6 hundreds and 2 ones, from 700, then the result is _______.
(a) 12 (b) 8
(c) 16 (d) 18

33. Which subtraction sentence gives same value as 17 – 7 ?
(a) 18 – 8 (b) 19 – 5
(c) 13 – 2 (d) 15 – 6

34. Golu had . He gave to his sister. How many are left with him?
(a)
(b)
(c)
(d)

35. There are – burst. How many are left?
(a) 3 (b) 2
(c) 1 (d) 4

36. 20 – 10 = ?
(a) 10 (b) 30
(c) 5 (d) 18

37. 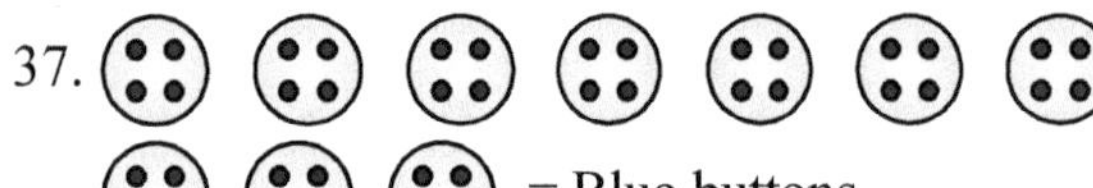
= Blue buttons

= Red buttons

How many more red buttons are needed so that red buttons are equal to blue buttons?

(a) 2 (b) 5
(c) 4 (d) 8

38. 
= ?

(a) 3 (b) 2
(c) 7 (d) 8

39. Which of the following is another way of 7 less than 10?

(a) 12 – 5 = 7 (b) 7 – 5 = 2
(c) 10 – 7 = 3 (d) 12 + 5 = 7

40. The difference between the greatest and the smallest number shown in the figure ________.

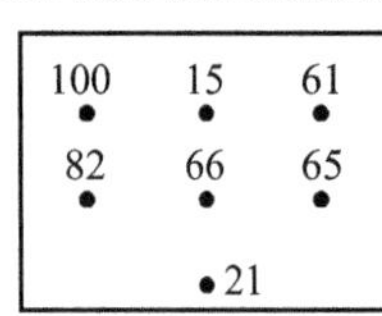

(a) 99 (b) 91
(c) 100 (d) 85

41. Which of the following has value less than 37?

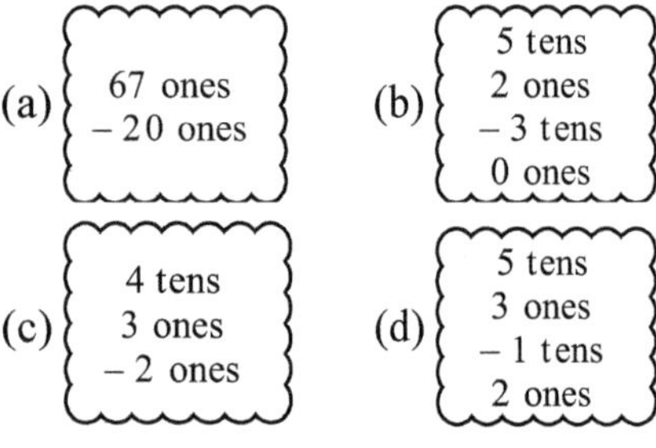

42. Which subtraction shows same value as

(a) 

(b) 

(c) 11 – 4

(d) 12 – 9

43. Which of the following options is incorrect?

(a) 17 – 17 = 0 (b) 38 – 16 = 22
(c) 73 – 31 = 32 (d) 87 – 25 = 62

44. Arun bought 37 candies. He gave 15 candies to his sister. How many candies are left with him?

(a) 12 (b) 32
(c) 22 (d) 26

45. There are 18 frogs in a pond. 7 of them jumped off. How many frogs are left in the pond?

(a) 18 – 7 = 11 (b) 18 – 7 = 13
(c) 18 – 7 = 12 (d) 18 – 7 = 10

46. Ria has 90 chocolates. She gave 23 chocolates to Neha and 42 chocolates to Minu. How many chocolates are left with her?

(a) 15 (b) 25
(c) 35 (d) 40

47. Which of the following is the correct form of writing 7 less than 19?

(a) 19 – 7 =12 (b) 19 – 12 = 7
(c) 19 + 7 = 26 (d) 12 – 7 = 5

48. Asha bought 45 cookies. She gave 23 cookies to her brother. How many cookies are left with her?

(a) 22 (b) 21
(c) 24 (d) 25

49. Choose the correct subtraction expression for the given picture?

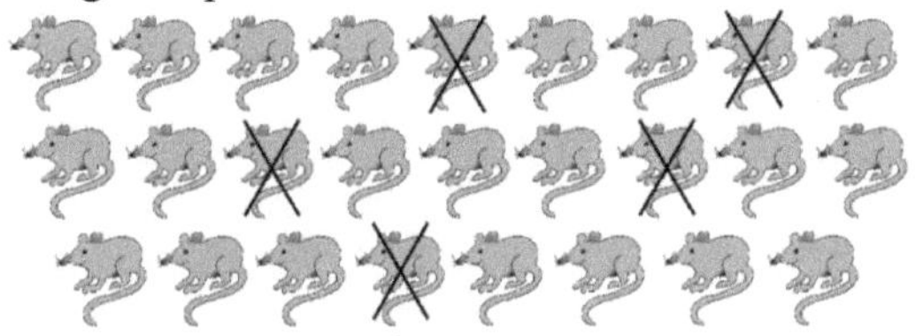

(a) 2 tens 6 ones – 5 ones
(b) 2 tens 7 ones – 5 ones
(c) 2 tens 6 ones – 4 ones
(d) 2 tens 5 ones – 5 ones

50. Which option shows difference between these two abacuses?

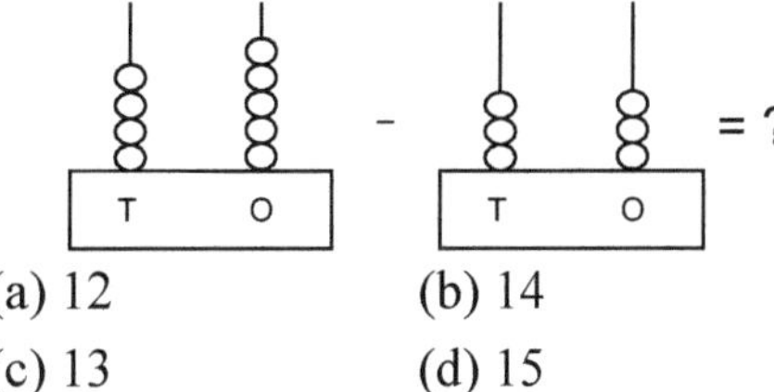

(a) 12 (b) 14
(c) 13 (d) 15

51. Find the value of M and N respectively.

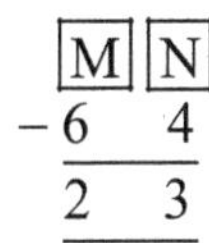

(a) 89 (b) 87
(c) 88 (d) 86

52. Which abacus shows (47 – 15)?

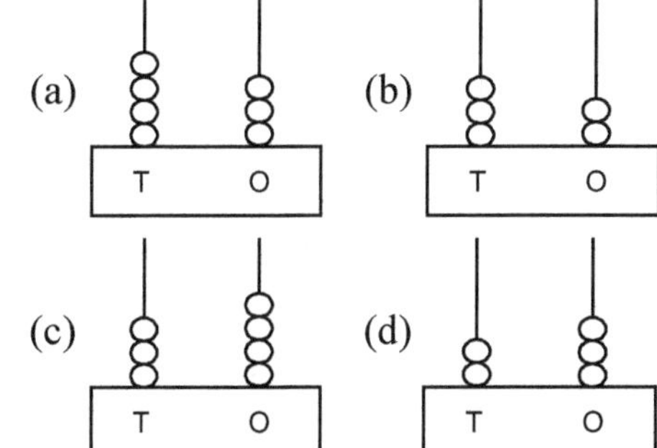

53. Which subtraction option gives same value as

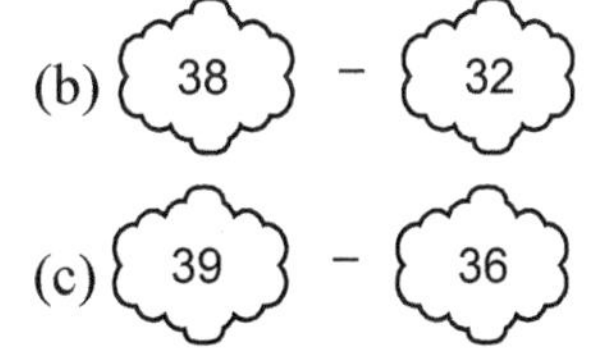

54. Which of the following number lines shows:

$7 - 3 = 4$

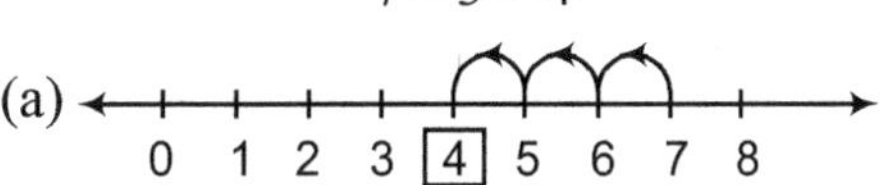

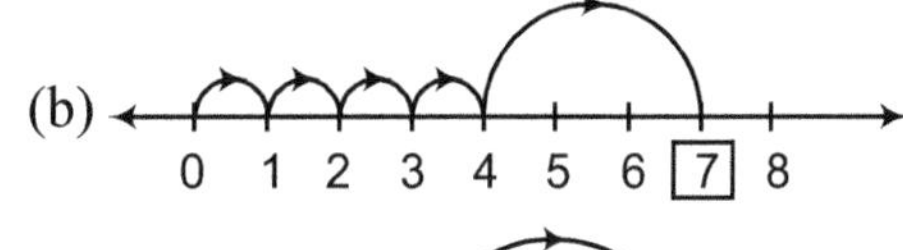

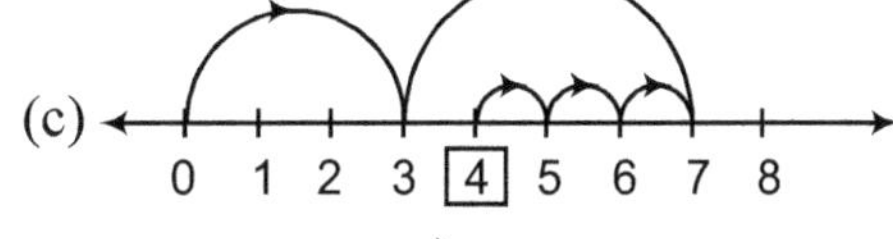

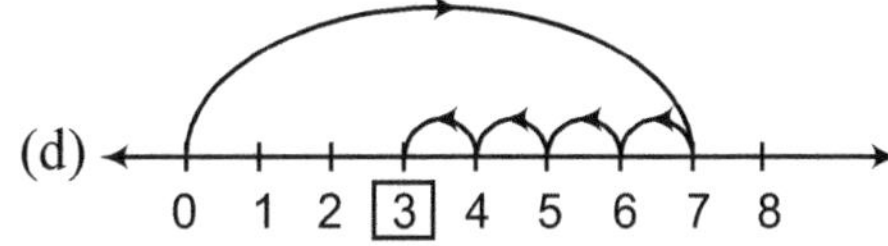

55. The number line represents _______.

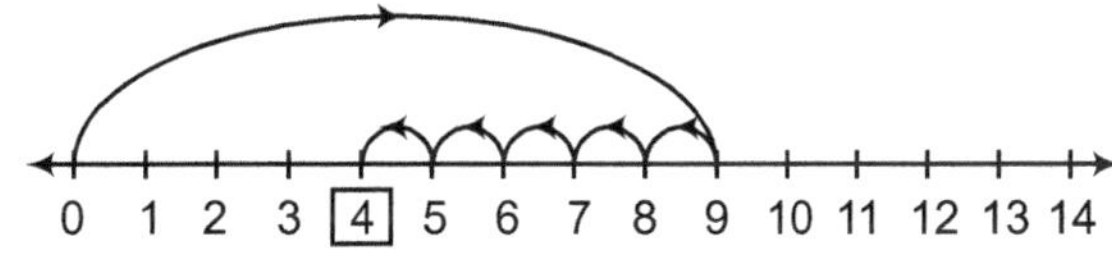

(a) 9 – 5 = 4 (b) 9 – 4 = 5
(c) 9 – 3 = 6 (d) 9 + 5 = 14

56. Which option shows the difference?

(a) 34 (b) 44
(c) 54 (d) 64

57. 5 tens 9 ones – 3 tens 7 ones = ?
(a) 22 (b) 12
(c) 32 (d) 26

58. What is the difference between the greatest and the smallest number shown in the box?

43	77	17	58
39	69	13	84
42	53	96	89

(a) 79 (b) 84
(c) 83 (d) 76

59. In the given circle the largest number is how much more than smallest number?

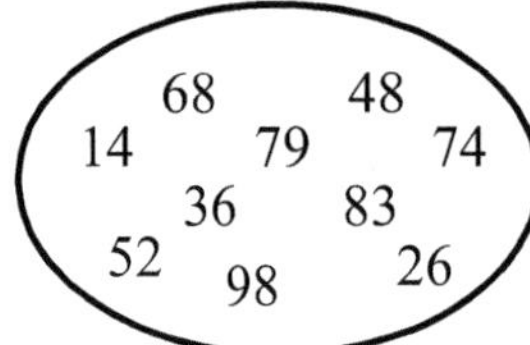

(a) 87 (b) 86
(c) 77 (d) 84

60. In the given box what is the difference between largest and second largest number?

43 92 69
58 74 53 84
86 34 96

(a) 4 (b) 6
(c) 10 (d) 12

Darken Your Choice with HB Pencil

1.	ⓐ	ⓑ	ⓒ	ⓓ	13.	ⓐ	ⓑ	ⓒ	ⓓ	25.	ⓐ	ⓑ	ⓒ	ⓓ	37.	ⓐ	ⓑ	ⓒ	ⓓ	49.	ⓐ	ⓑ	ⓒ	ⓓ
2.	ⓐ	ⓑ	ⓒ	ⓓ	14.	ⓐ	ⓑ	ⓒ	ⓓ	26.	ⓐ	ⓑ	ⓒ	ⓓ	38.	ⓐ	ⓑ	ⓒ	ⓓ	50.	ⓐ	ⓑ	ⓒ	ⓓ
3.	ⓐ	ⓑ	ⓒ	ⓓ	15.	ⓐ	ⓑ	ⓒ	ⓓ	27.	ⓐ	ⓑ	ⓒ	ⓓ	39.	ⓐ	ⓑ	ⓒ	ⓓ	51.	ⓐ	ⓑ	ⓒ	ⓓ
4.	ⓐ	ⓑ	ⓒ	ⓓ	16.	ⓐ	ⓑ	ⓒ	ⓓ	28.	ⓐ	ⓑ	ⓒ	ⓓ	40.	ⓐ	ⓑ	ⓒ	ⓓ	52.	ⓐ	ⓑ	ⓒ	ⓓ
5.	ⓐ	ⓑ	ⓒ	ⓓ	17.	ⓐ	ⓑ	ⓒ	ⓓ	29.	ⓐ	ⓑ	ⓒ	ⓓ	41.	ⓐ	ⓑ	ⓒ	ⓓ	53.	ⓐ	ⓑ	ⓒ	ⓓ
6.	ⓐ	ⓑ	ⓒ	ⓓ	18.	ⓐ	ⓑ	ⓒ	ⓓ	30.	ⓐ	ⓑ	ⓒ	ⓓ	42.	ⓐ	ⓑ	ⓒ	ⓓ	54.	ⓐ	ⓑ	ⓒ	ⓓ
7.	ⓐ	ⓑ	ⓒ	ⓓ	19.	ⓐ	ⓑ	ⓒ	ⓓ	31.	ⓐ	ⓑ	ⓒ	ⓓ	43.	ⓐ	ⓑ	ⓒ	ⓓ	55.	ⓐ	ⓑ	ⓒ	ⓓ
8.	ⓐ	ⓑ	ⓒ	ⓓ	20.	ⓐ	ⓑ	ⓒ	ⓓ	32.	ⓐ	ⓑ	ⓒ	ⓓ	44.	ⓐ	ⓑ	ⓒ	ⓓ	56.	ⓐ	ⓑ	ⓒ	ⓓ
9.	ⓐ	ⓑ	ⓒ	ⓓ	21.	ⓐ	ⓑ	ⓒ	ⓓ	33.	ⓐ	ⓑ	ⓒ	ⓓ	45.	ⓐ	ⓑ	ⓒ	ⓓ	57.	ⓐ	ⓑ	ⓒ	ⓓ
10.	ⓐ	ⓑ	ⓒ	ⓓ	22.	ⓐ	ⓑ	ⓒ	ⓓ	34.	ⓐ	ⓑ	ⓒ	ⓓ	46.	ⓐ	ⓑ	ⓒ	ⓓ	58.	ⓐ	ⓑ	ⓒ	ⓓ
11.	ⓐ	ⓑ	ⓒ	ⓓ	23.	ⓐ	ⓑ	ⓒ	ⓓ	35.	ⓐ	ⓑ	ⓒ	ⓓ	47.	ⓐ	ⓑ	ⓒ	ⓓ	59.	ⓐ	ⓑ	ⓒ	ⓓ
12.	ⓐ	ⓑ	ⓒ	ⓓ	24.	ⓐ	ⓑ	ⓒ	ⓓ	36.	ⓐ	ⓑ	ⓒ	ⓓ	48.	ⓐ	ⓑ	ⓒ	ⓓ	60.	ⓐ	ⓑ	ⓒ	ⓓ

WORKBOOK

Measurement

- The distance between two points is called length. The standard unit of length is metre.

1 metre = 100 centimetres

- Metre is used to measure the length of a piece of cloth, the height of a door as well as the height of a room.
- Heaviness of an object is called mass, which is usually called weight.
- Weight of an object can be measured by comparing it with the weight of a known object.
- To represent accurate weight we use units such as kilogram and gram. Kilogram is written as kg and gram is written as gm.

1 kilogram = 1000 grams

- The amount of space inside an object is called capacity.
- We use standard units such as litre and millilitre to measure capacity. Litre is written as *l* and millilitre is written as *ml*.

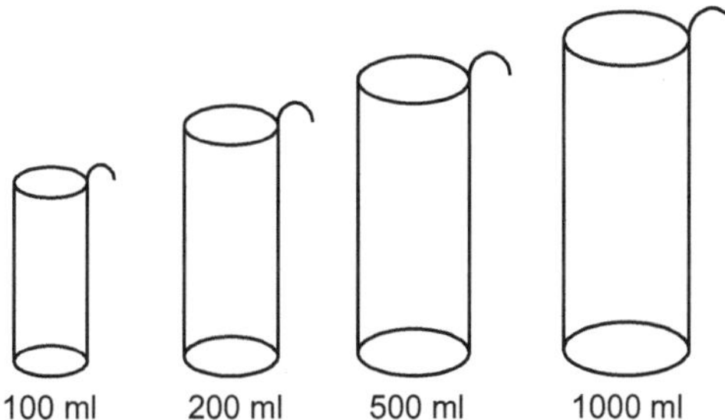

- Liquids in small quantities are measured in milliliters. Liquids are measured using special vessels.
- In short centimeter is written as cm and metre is written as m.

1 kilometer = 1000 metres

Multiple Choice Questions

1. Which of the following is the largest?
   (a) 38 (b) 15
   (c) 35 (d) 25
2. Which cone is the biggest?
   (a) (b)
   (c) (d)
3. Which of the following is the smallest square?
   (a) (b)
   (c) (d)
4. Which of the following is the lightest?
   (a) Ink-pot (b) Pencil
   (c) Book (d) Bag
5. Ft is the abbreviation for which of the following units of measurement?
   (a) Feet (b) Ounces
   (c) Inches (d) Yards
6. What three measurements do you need to determine the volume of a rectangular box?
   (a) Width, height, weight
   (b) Length, width, height
   (c) Length, Width, circumference
   (d) Width, weight, distance
7. How many millimeters are in 50 cm?
   (a) 100 (b) 500
   (c) 5000 (d) 50000
8. Which unit of measurement would be the best to use to calculate the length of a long car journey?
   (a) Centimetres (b) Millimetres
   (c) Both (a) and (b) (d) Kilometres
9. How many grams are in 1 kg?
   (a) 10 g (b) 100 g
   (c) 1000 g (d) 10000 g
10. 1 dime is equal to how many cents?
    (a) 15 cents (b) 10 cents
    (c) 12 cents (d) 25 cents
11. Which is a better estimate for the weight of an ice cube?
    (a) 30 grams (b) 30 kilograms
    (c) (a) and (b) both (d) None of these
12. Which is better estimate for the volume of a soda bottle cap?
    (a) 17 litres (b) 17 millilitres
    (c) (a) and (b) both (d) None of these
13. Which is more, 1 litre or 1000 millilitres?
    (a) 1 litre
    (b) 1000 millilitres
    (c) Neither. They are equal
    (d) None of these
14. ______ milligrams = 1 gram.
    (a) 1000 (b) 100
    (c) 10 (d) 10000
15. Which is a better estimate for the distance of a day-long hike?
    (a) 14 kilometres (b) 14 Millimeters
    (c) (a) and (b) both (d) None of these
16. Which is a better estimate for the length of an alligator?
    (a) 4 metres (b) 4 centimetres
    (c) 4 kilometres (d) both (a) and (b)
17. What is the total weight of these four packages?

    10 kg 20 kg 17 kg 13 kg

    (a) 60 kg (b) 50 kg
    (c) 70 kg (d) 65 kg

18. Ravi is 20 years old. What was his age 8 years back?
(a) 11 (b) 12
(c) 13 (d) 14

19. How much is 7,918 smaller than 10,000?
(a) 2082 (b) 2182
(c) 3082 (d) 2282

Direction (20–25) : Look at the figures below and answer the given questions:

40 m
30 m
68 m

20. The tree is _______ m tall.
(a) 30 m (b) 70 m
(c) 35 m (d) 40 m

21. The air conditioner is _______ m tall.
(a) 30 m (b) 70 m
(c) 40 m (d) 68 m

22. The bookshelf is __ m tall.
(a) 60 m (b) 30 m
(c) 68 m (d) 72 m

23. The total height of the tree and air conditioner is _______.
(a) 30 m (b) 70 m
(c) 32 m (d) 98 m

24. The total height of all three is _______.
(a) 176 m (b) 132 m
(c) 170 m (d) 138 m

25. The bookshelf is ______ m taller than air conditioner.
(a) 28 m (b) 25 m
(c) 38 m (d) 45 m

Direction (26–33) : See the given figures and answer the following questions.

Yam
5 kg
Carrot
1 kg
Jackfruit
8 kg

26. The mass of yam is ______ kg.
(a) 5 (b) 7
(c) 1 (d) 8

27. The mass of carrot is ______ g.
(a) 15 g (b) 1 g
(c) 8 g (d) 1000 g

28. The mass of jackfruit is _______ g.
(a) 150 g (b) 180 g
(c) 8000 g (d) 8 g

29. The mass of jackfruit is _______ kg more than yam.
(a) 3 kg (b) 4 kg
(c) 7 kg (d) 5 kg

30. The total mass of yam and carrot is ______ kg.
(a) 7 kg (b) 6 kg
(c) 10 kg (d) 8 kg

31. The total mass of jackfruit and carrot is ______ kg.
(a) 7 kg (b) 6 kg
(c) 9 kg (d) 19 kg

32. The total mass of all three vegetables is _____ g.
(a) 14000 (b) 5000
(c) 9000 (d) 8000

33. The mass of yam is ______ kg more than carrot.
(a) 7 kg (b) 4 kg
(c) 12 kg (d) 8 kg

34. Which of these is lighter than a book?
(a) Table (b) Car
(c) Aeroplane (d) Pencil

35. Which of the two cylinders have same height?

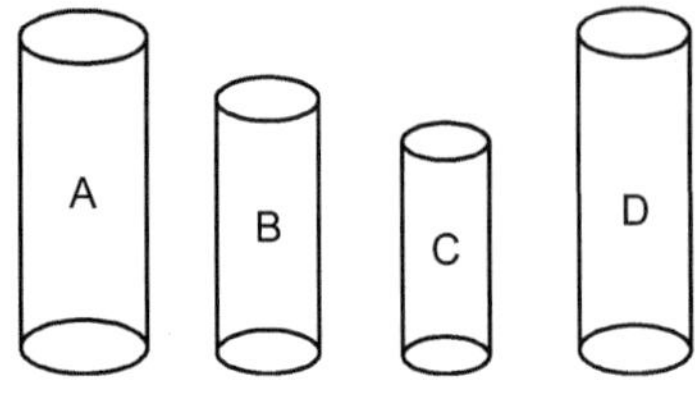

(a) A and D (b) B and C
(c) A and C (d) C and D

36. Which of the following has the least capacity?

(a) Bottle (b) Mug
(c) Kettle (d) Basket

37. Which cone is the shortest?

(a) 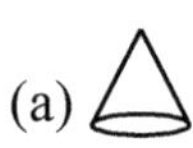 (b) 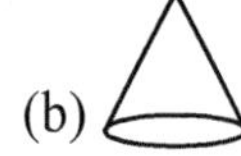

(c) 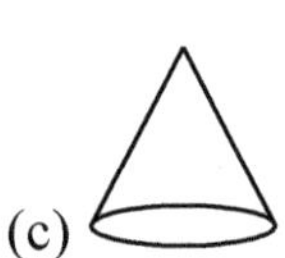 (d) 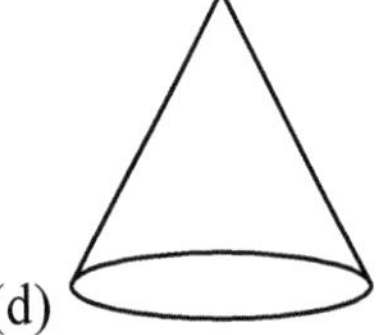

38. Which of the following is the smallest?

(a) 17 (b) 32
(c) 38 (d) 40

39. $\frac{1}{2}$ kilogram = _______ grams.

(a) 50 grams (b) 5000 grams
(c) 500 grams (d) 1000 grams

40. 1 metre = _______.

(a) 100 cm (b) 200 cm
(c) 250 cm (d) 400 cm

41. Sonu's weight is 28 kg. Rohit's weight is 5 kg less than Sonu's weight. What is the weight of Rohit?

(a) 33 kg (b) 23 kg
(c) 24 kg (d) 25 kg

42. A bag of flour weighs 4 kg. How much will 5 such bags of flour weigh?

(a) 10 kg (b) 12 kg
(c) 16 kg (d) 20 kg

43. The weight of Ria's doll is equal to 10 marbles. What will be the weight of two such dolls?

(a) 2 marbles (b) 10 marbles
(c) 5 marbles (d) 20 marbles

44. Nancy has following two combs.

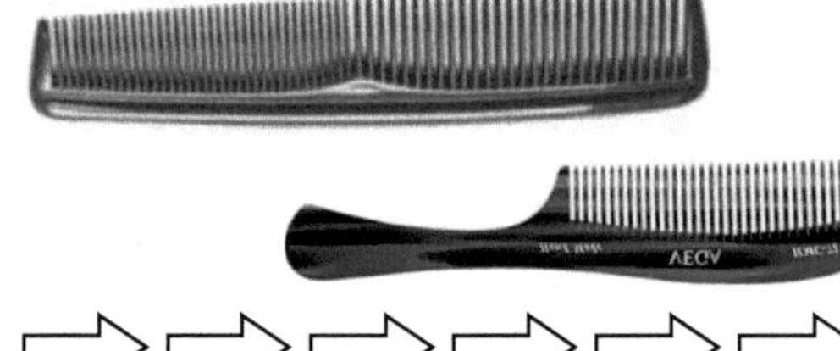

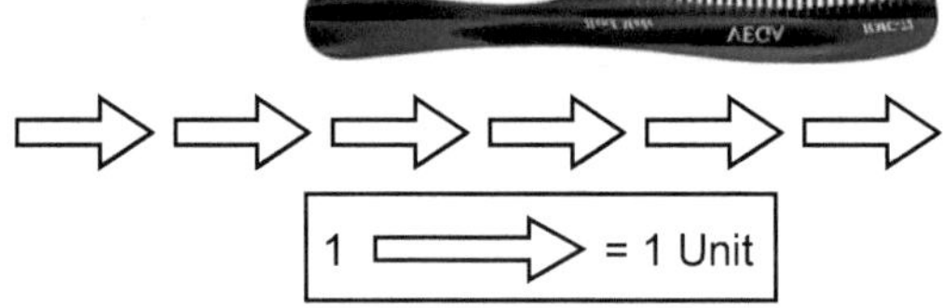

What is the total length of both the combs.

(a) 7 units (b) 8 units
(c) 9 units (d) 10 units

45. Which of the following is the heaviest?

(a) (b)
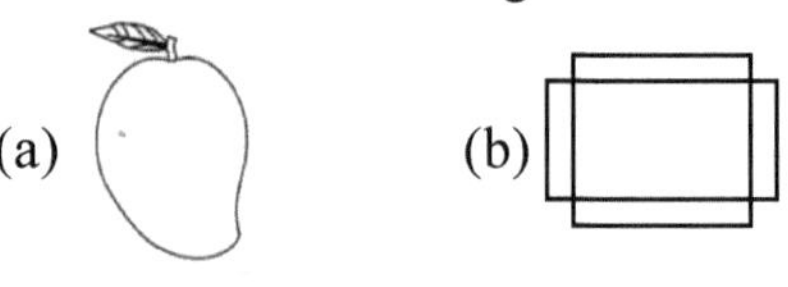

(c)  (d) 

46. If 1 ⇨ means 2 units, then what is the length of gun?

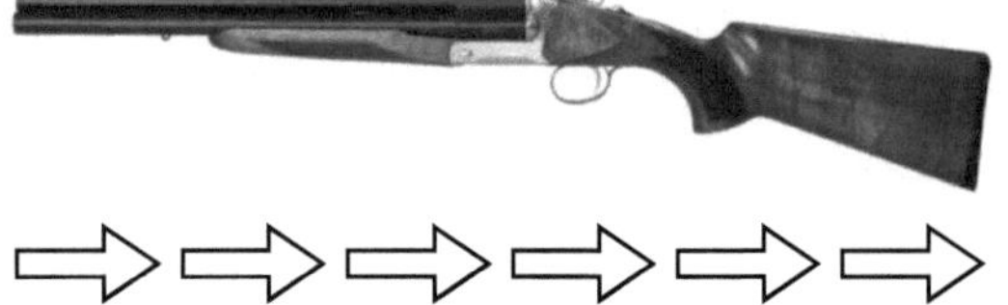

(a) 10 units (b) 12 units
(c) 14 units (d) 16 units

47. Tape is .... span long

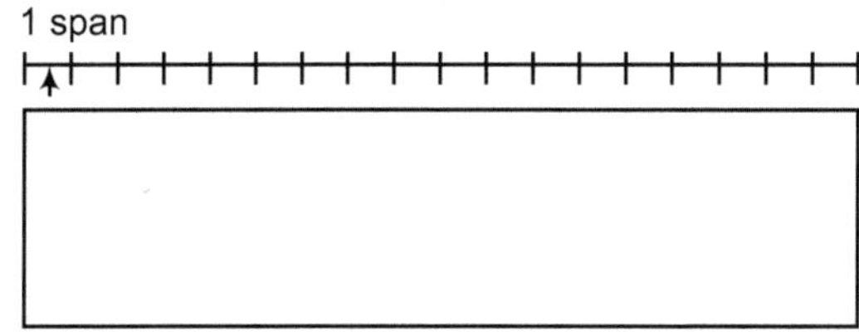

(a) 17 (b) 16

(c) 18 (d) 15

48. Which of the following strips is as long as the pencil?

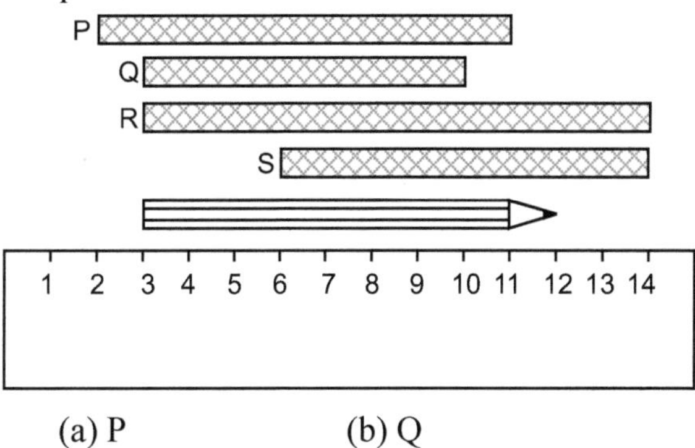

(a) P (b) Q

(c) R (d) S

49. In the given figure, who is taller than Mini and shorter than Nilu?

(a) Raju (b) Monu

(c) Nilu (d) Rani

50. Which balloon has longest string?

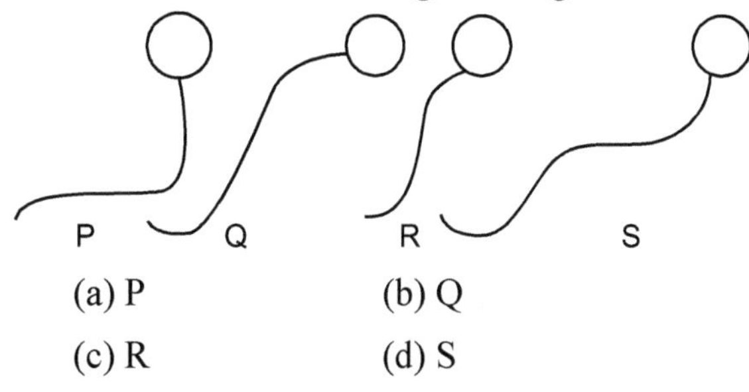

(a) P (b) Q

(c) R (d) S

Darken Your Choice with HB Pencil

1.	ⓐ	ⓑ	ⓒ	ⓓ	11.	ⓐ	ⓑ	ⓒ	ⓓ	21.	ⓐ	ⓑ	ⓒ	ⓓ	31.	ⓐ	ⓑ	ⓒ	ⓓ	41.	ⓐ	ⓑ	ⓒ	ⓓ
2.	ⓐ	ⓑ	ⓒ	ⓓ	12.	ⓐ	ⓑ	ⓒ	ⓓ	22.	ⓐ	ⓑ	ⓒ	ⓓ	32.	ⓐ	ⓑ	ⓒ	ⓓ	42.	ⓐ	ⓑ	ⓒ	ⓓ
3.	ⓐ	ⓑ	ⓒ	ⓓ	13.	ⓐ	ⓑ	ⓒ	ⓓ	23.	ⓐ	ⓑ	ⓒ	ⓓ	33.	ⓐ	ⓑ	ⓒ	ⓓ	43.	ⓐ	ⓑ	ⓒ	ⓓ
4.	ⓐ	ⓑ	ⓒ	ⓓ	14.	ⓐ	ⓑ	ⓒ	ⓓ	24.	ⓐ	ⓑ	ⓒ	ⓓ	34.	ⓐ	ⓑ	ⓒ	ⓓ	44.	ⓐ	ⓑ	ⓒ	ⓓ
5.	ⓐ	ⓑ	ⓒ	ⓓ	15.	ⓐ	ⓑ	ⓒ	ⓓ	25.	ⓐ	ⓑ	ⓒ	ⓓ	35.	ⓐ	ⓑ	ⓒ	ⓓ	45.	ⓐ	ⓑ	ⓒ	ⓓ
6.	ⓐ	ⓑ	ⓒ	ⓓ	16.	ⓐ	ⓑ	ⓒ	ⓓ	26.	ⓐ	ⓑ	ⓒ	ⓓ	36.	ⓐ	ⓑ	ⓒ	ⓓ	46.	ⓐ	ⓑ	ⓒ	ⓓ
7.	ⓐ	ⓑ	ⓒ	ⓓ	17.	ⓐ	ⓑ	ⓒ	ⓓ	27.	ⓐ	ⓑ	ⓒ	ⓓ	37.	ⓐ	ⓑ	ⓒ	ⓓ	47.	ⓐ	ⓑ	ⓒ	ⓓ
8.	ⓐ	ⓑ	ⓒ	ⓓ	18.	ⓐ	ⓑ	ⓒ	ⓓ	28.	ⓐ	ⓑ	ⓒ	ⓓ	38.	ⓐ	ⓑ	ⓒ	ⓓ	48.	ⓐ	ⓑ	ⓒ	ⓓ
9.	ⓐ	ⓑ	ⓒ	ⓓ	19.	ⓐ	ⓑ	ⓒ	ⓓ	29.	ⓐ	ⓑ	ⓒ	ⓓ	39.	ⓐ	ⓑ	ⓒ	ⓓ	49.	ⓐ	ⓑ	ⓒ	ⓓ
10.	ⓐ	ⓑ	ⓒ	ⓓ	20.	ⓐ	ⓑ	ⓒ	ⓓ	30.	ⓐ	ⓑ	ⓒ	ⓓ	40.	ⓐ	ⓑ	ⓒ	ⓓ	50.	ⓐ	ⓑ	ⓒ	ⓓ

WORKBOOK

5 Time

- Time is measured using a clock. A clock has numbers 1 to 12 on its face, a short hand called the hour hand and a long hand called the minute hand.

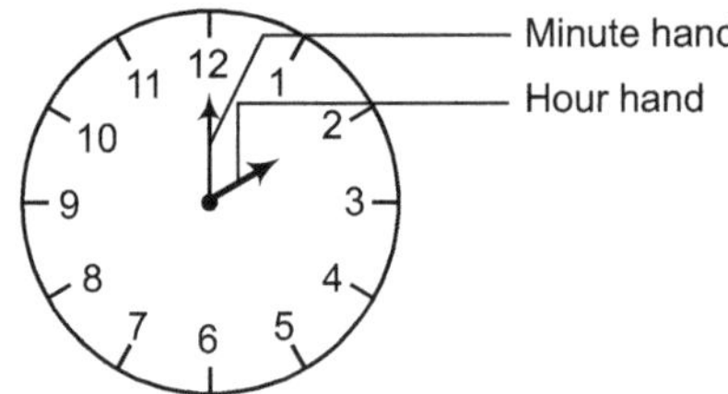

- We use am for time from 12 midnight to just before noon.
- We use pm for time from 12 noon to just before midnight.
- We use 2 dots (:) to separate hours and minutes.
- When the hour hand is at 5 and the minute hand is at 12, the time is read as 5 O'clock or 5 : 00
- 24 hours of a day are divided into day and night.
- The time between 12 O' clock in the day and 12'o clock in the night is called afternoon.
- There are seven days in a weak :
  Monday, Tuesday, Wednesday, Thursday, Friday, Saturday, Sunday.
- Calendar is a chart which shows days, weeks and months of a year. There are 12 months in a year.

Month	Days
January	31
February	28/29
March	31
April	30
May	31
June	30
July	31
August	31
September	30
October	31

November	30
December	31

- There are seven months which have 31 days each.
- The years in which February has 29 days is called a leap year.

1 Leap year = 366 days.

1 year = 365 days.

Multiple Choice Questions

1. Which day comes just before Tuesday?
   (a) Monday (b) Wednesday
   (c) Thursday (d) Sunday
2. How many days are there in 5 weeks?
   (a) 45 (b) 42
   (c) 35 (d) 46
3. Which of the following clocks shows time as 6'o clock?
   (a) 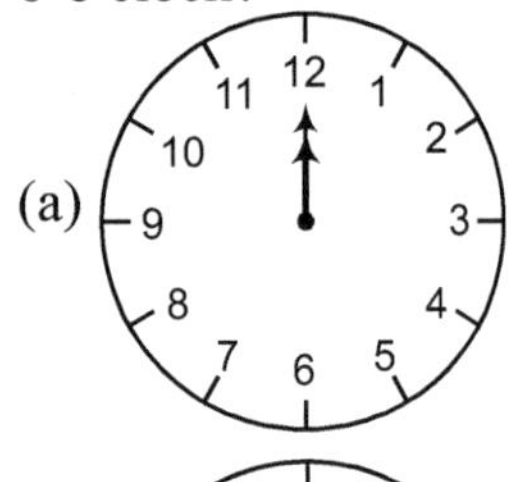
   (b) 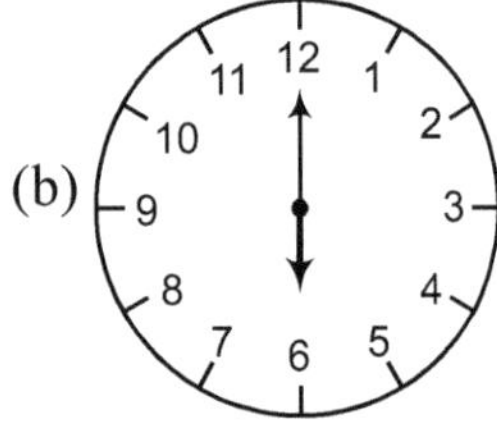
   (c) 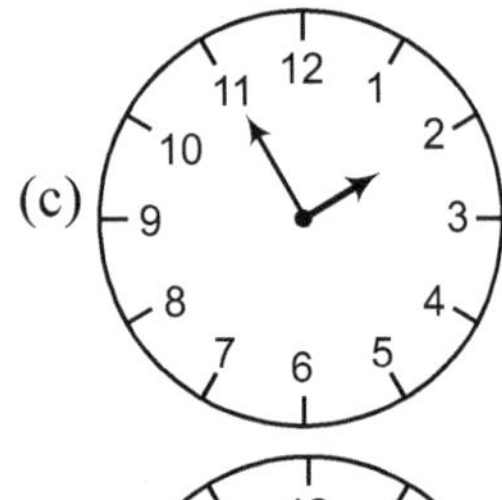
   (d) 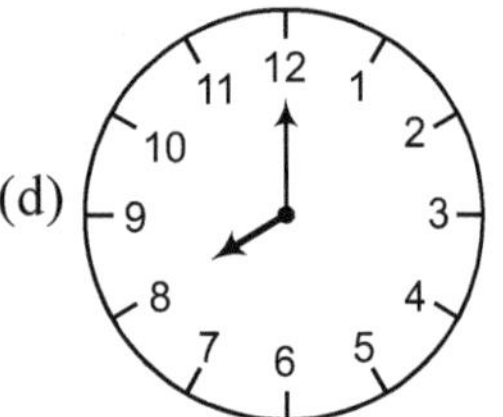
4. Ravi takes 5 minutes to draw a bag. How long does he take to draw 4 similar bags?
   (a) 20 min (b) 22 min
   (c) 30 min (d) 28 min
5. How many minutes are there in one day?
   (a) 1250 (b) 1440
   (c) 1140 (d) 2440
6. How many days are there in February 2016?
   (a) 28 (b) 29
   (c) 30 (d) 31
7. The month with 30 days is _______.
   (a) December (b) January
   (c) March (d) April
8. The minute hand takes ___ minutes to move from 4 to 8.
   (a) 10 (b) 20
   (c) 30 (d) 40
9. Which of the following clocks shows time less than 8'o clock?

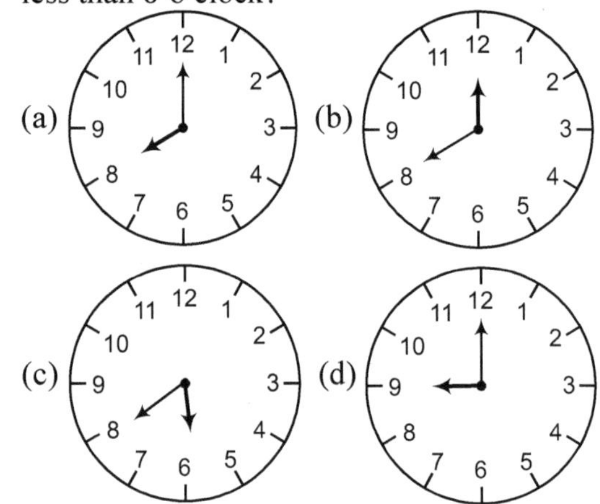

10. Which of the following clocks shows time equal to 9'o clock.

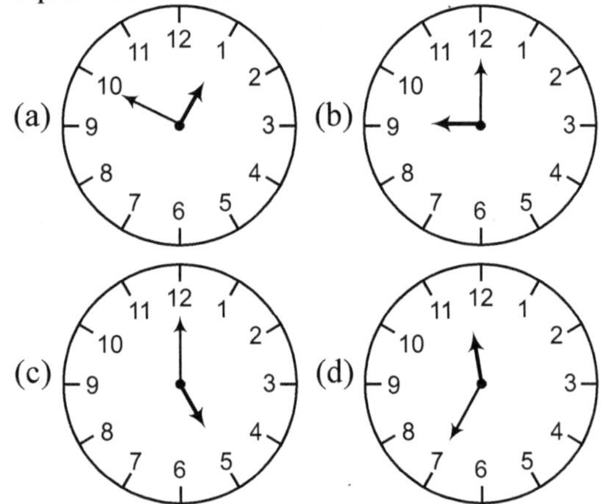

11. How many months of a year has 30 days?
    (a) 4 (b) 7
    (c) 5 (d) 6

12. When do you wake up?
(a) Afternoon (b) Night
(c) Morning (d) Evening

13. Which of the following clocks shows 11'o clock?

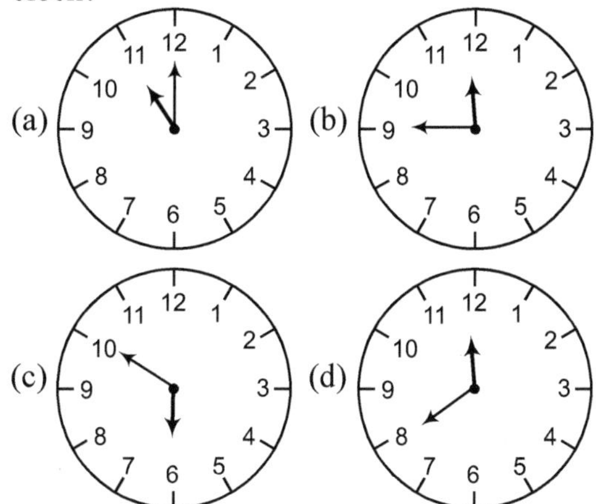

14. 1 leap year = ______ days.
(a) 364 (b) 365
(c) 366 (d) 370

15. If today is Monday, then yesterday was _____.
(a) Tuesday (b) Sunday
(c) Wednesday (d) Thursday.

16. The month with neither 31 days nor 30 days is _______.
(a) April (b) February
(c) July (d) May

17. Which of the following clocks shows 10 : 30?

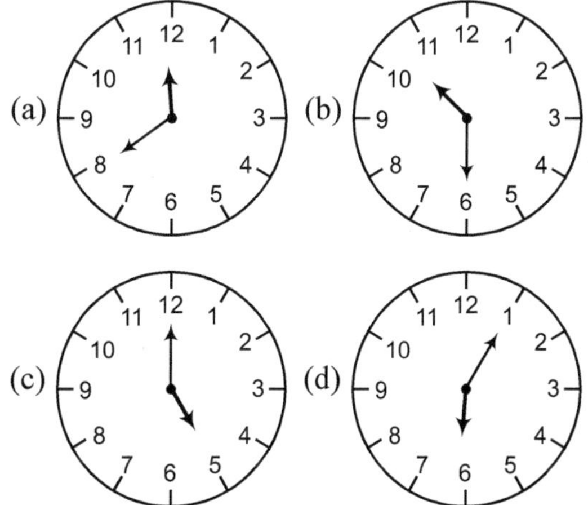

18. You play with your friends in playground in the _______.
(a) Evening (b) Night
(c) Morning (d) Day

19. 96 hours is equal to _______.
(a) 4 days 3 hours (b) 5 days 2 hours
(c) 4 days 6 hours (d) 4 days

20. The minute hand takes ______ minutes to move from 2 to 4.
(a) 5 (b) 10
(c) 15 (d) 20

21. The hour hand takes ______ hours to move from 2 to 5.
(a) 1 (b) 2
(c) 3 (d) 6

22. 240 seconds is equal to _______.
(a) 7 min (b) 3 min
(c) 8 min (d) 4 min

23. 256 minutes is equal to _______.
(a) 5 hours 3 min (b) 3 hours 12 min
(c) 4 hours 16 min (d) 2 hours 10 min

24. Raju was born on 29th of February. His birthday comes _______.
(a) After every three years
(b) Twice in a year
(c) After every four years
(d) After every two years

25. When the short hand is at 11 and the long hand is at 12, the time is _______.
(a) 12'o clock (b) 11'o clock
(c) 9'o clock (d) 10' o clock

26. Which day comes just after Friday?
(a) Saturday (b) Sunday
(c) Monday (d) Tuesday

27. How many days are there in 8 weeks?
(a) 56 days (b) 54 days
(c) 52 days (d) 34 days

28. My sister and I played a game for 14 minutes. We started at 3 : 26. What time did we stop?
(a) 3 : 00 (b) 3 : 40
(c) 4 : 04 (d) 3 : 30

29. Ravi went to a movie that started at 2 : 45 and ended at 4 : 15. How long was the movie?
(a) 2 hours
(b) 3 hours
(c) 1 hour 30 minutes
(d) 4 hours

30. What time is it on the clock?

(a) 3 : 05 (b) 6 : 14
(c) 2 : 14 (d) 1 : 15

31. If someone says it is midnight that means it is _______.
(a) 12 : 00 noon (b) 12 : 01 am
(c) 12 : 00 night (d) 12 : 01 pm

32. A quarter to 5 means _______.
(a) 4 : 45 (b) 5 : 15
(c) 4 : 25 (d) 5 : 25

33. It is 3 : 00 pm now. What will be the time after 3 hours?
(a) 6 : 00 am (b) 6 : 00 pm
(c) 7 : 00 pm (d) 8 : 00 am

34. A pet store opens at 7 : 00 am and closes at 5 : 00 pm. How long is the store open?
(a) 8 hours (b) 10 hours
(c) 6 hours (d) None of these

35. How many seconds are there in a minute?
(a) 45 (b) 35
(c) 54 (d) 60

36. How many minutes are there in a quarter of an hour?
(a) 15 (b) 30
(c) 60 (d) 55

37. How many minutes are there in half an hour?
(a) 15 (b) 30
(c) 35 (d) 60

38. 1 hour and 25 minutes = _____ minutes.
(a) 65 (b) 75
(c) 85 (d) 35

39. A play starts at 7 : 30 pm and lasts until 9 : 00 pm. How long is the play?
(a) 1 hour 30 minutes
(b) 2 hours
(c) 1 hour 15 minutes
(d) 1 hour 45 minutes

40. How many minutes are there in seven hours?
(a) 700 minutes (b) 400 minutes
(c) 420 minutes (d) 490 minutes

41. Which day of the week is always a holiday?
(a) Saturday (b) Friday
(c) Sunday (d) Tuesday

42. Which is the 7th month of a year?
(a) June (b) July
(c) August (d) November

43. In the year 2017, February had ___ days?
(a) 28 (b) 29
(c) 30 (d) 31

44. How many months of a year have 31 days?
(a) 5 (b) 6
(c) 7 (d) 4

45. How many months lie between second and tenth month of a year?
(a) 4 (b) 5
(c) 6 (d) 7

46. Which of the following months comes just before the 11th month of a year?
(a) September (b) October
(c) November (d) December

47. Which of the following activities can be done in 1 minute?
   (a) Playing cricket (b) Eating a bread
   (c) Painting a wall (d) Going to school

48. If a month has 28 days, then how many weeks will be there in that month?
   (a) 2 (b) 3
   (c) 5 (d) 4

49. Which of the following months comes between June and October?
   (a) March (b) May
   (c) September (d) December

50. How many weeks are there in a leap year?
   (a) 51 (b) 52
   (c) 53 (d) 50

51. Which of the following months comes after March and before August?
   (a) May (b) November
   (c) October (d) September

52. How many days are there in 7 weeks?
   (a) 56 (b) 42
   (c) 49 (d) 35

53. If today is Monday, then the day before yesterday was _______.
   (a) Friday (b) Tuesday
   (c) Sunday (d) Saturday

54. Which of the following months is the 6th month of a year?
   (a) May (b) June
   (c) March (d) July

55. Which of the following activities do you do in the morning?
   (a) Playing
   (b) Bathing
   (c) Sleeping
   (d) Coming home from school

56. If day before yesterday was Thursday, then day after tomorrow will be _______.
   (a) Monday (b) Sunday
   (c) Friday (d) Saturday

57. If a month has 31 days. How many days are there in 3 such months?
   (a) 62 (b) 93
   (c) 94 (d) 96

58. Which of the following months is in between September and November?
   (a) October (b) December
   (c) September (d) August

59. We go to bed when stars are shining in the sky. It must be _______.
   (a) Night (b) Evening
   (c) Morning (d) Afternoon

☺☺☺

Darken Your Choice with HB Pencil

1.	ⓐ	ⓑ	ⓒ	ⓓ	13.	ⓐ	ⓑ	ⓒ	ⓓ	25.	ⓐ	ⓑ	ⓒ	ⓓ	37.	ⓐ	ⓑ	ⓒ	ⓓ	49.	ⓐ	ⓑ	ⓒ	ⓓ
2.	ⓐ	ⓑ	ⓒ	ⓓ	14.	ⓐ	ⓑ	ⓒ	ⓓ	26.	ⓐ	ⓑ	ⓒ	ⓓ	38.	ⓐ	ⓑ	ⓒ	ⓓ	50.	ⓐ	ⓑ	ⓒ	ⓓ
3.	ⓐ	ⓑ	ⓒ	ⓓ	15.	ⓐ	ⓑ	ⓒ	ⓓ	27.	ⓐ	ⓑ	ⓒ	ⓓ	39.	ⓐ	ⓑ	ⓒ	ⓓ	51.	ⓐ	ⓑ	ⓒ	ⓓ
4.	ⓐ	ⓑ	ⓒ	ⓓ	16.	ⓐ	ⓑ	ⓒ	ⓓ	28.	ⓐ	ⓑ	ⓒ	ⓓ	40.	ⓐ	ⓑ	ⓒ	ⓓ	52.	ⓐ	ⓑ	ⓒ	ⓓ
5.	ⓐ	ⓑ	ⓒ	ⓓ	17.	ⓐ	ⓑ	ⓒ	ⓓ	29.	ⓐ	ⓑ	ⓒ	ⓓ	41.	ⓐ	ⓑ	ⓒ	ⓓ	53.	ⓐ	ⓑ	ⓒ	ⓓ
6.	ⓐ	ⓑ	ⓒ	ⓓ	18.	ⓐ	ⓑ	ⓒ	ⓓ	30.	ⓐ	ⓑ	ⓒ	ⓓ	42.	ⓐ	ⓑ	ⓒ	ⓓ	54.	ⓐ	ⓑ	ⓒ	ⓓ
7.	ⓐ	ⓑ	ⓒ	ⓓ	19.	ⓐ	ⓑ	ⓒ	ⓓ	31.	ⓐ	ⓑ	ⓒ	ⓓ	43.	ⓐ	ⓑ	ⓒ	ⓓ	55.	ⓐ	ⓑ	ⓒ	ⓓ
8.	ⓐ	ⓑ	ⓒ	ⓓ	20.	ⓐ	ⓑ	ⓒ	ⓓ	32.	ⓐ	ⓑ	ⓒ	ⓓ	44.	ⓐ	ⓑ	ⓒ	ⓓ	56.	ⓐ	ⓑ	ⓒ	ⓓ
9.	ⓐ	ⓑ	ⓒ	ⓓ	21.	ⓐ	ⓑ	ⓒ	ⓓ	33.	ⓐ	ⓑ	ⓒ	ⓓ	45.	ⓐ	ⓑ	ⓒ	ⓓ	57.	ⓐ	ⓑ	ⓒ	ⓓ
10.	ⓐ	ⓑ	ⓒ	ⓓ	22.	ⓐ	ⓑ	ⓒ	ⓓ	34.	ⓐ	ⓑ	ⓒ	ⓓ	46.	ⓐ	ⓑ	ⓒ	ⓓ	58.	ⓐ	ⓑ	ⓒ	ⓓ
11.	ⓐ	ⓑ	ⓒ	ⓓ	23.	ⓐ	ⓑ	ⓒ	ⓓ	35.	ⓐ	ⓑ	ⓒ	ⓓ	47.	ⓐ	ⓑ	ⓒ	ⓓ	59.	ⓐ	ⓑ	ⓒ	ⓓ
12.	ⓐ	ⓑ	ⓒ	ⓓ	24.	ⓐ	ⓑ	ⓒ	ⓓ	36.	ⓐ	ⓑ	ⓒ	ⓓ	48.	ⓐ	ⓑ	ⓒ	ⓓ					

WORKBOOK

6 Money

- Money is used for buying the things that we need. In India, money is counted in rupees and paise.
- Money is also known as currency.
- Symbol of Indian rupees is

- 1 Rupee = 100 Paise
- The paper based notes available in India are of ₹ 2000, ₹ 500, ₹ 100, ₹ 50, ₹ 20, ₹ 10, ₹ 5.
- 1 rupee = 100 paise
- 100 rupees = 10 notes of 10 rupees
- 500 rupees note = 50 notes of 10 rupees
  = 25 notes of 20 rupees
  = 10 notes of 50 rupees
  = 5 notes of 100 rupees
- 2000 rupees note = 200 notes of 10 rupees
  = 100 notes of 20 rupees
  = 40 notes of 50 rupees
  = 20 notes of 100 rupees
  = 4 notes of 500 rupees

Multiple Choice Questions

1. Put these amounts of money in order from smallest to largest.
   ₹ 2.16, ₹ 2.42, ₹ 2.50, ₹ 2.18, ₹ 2.66.
   (a) ₹ 2.16, ₹ 2.18, ₹ 2.42, ₹ 2.50, ₹ 2.66
   (b) ₹ 2.42, ₹ 2.50, ₹ 2.18, ₹ 2.66, ₹ 2.16
   (c) ₹ 2.18, ₹ 2.42, ₹ 2.50, ₹ 2.18, ₹ 2.66
   (d) None of these
2. What is ₹ 89 rounded to the nearest 10?
   (a) ₹ 90 (b) ₹ 70
   (c) ₹ 100 (d) ₹ 80
3. What is ₹ 382 rounded to the nearest 100?
   (a) ₹ 300 (b) ₹ 380
   (c) ₹ 400 (d) ₹ 500
4. If one pen costs ₹. 20, how much does Rakesh have to pay for 3 pens?
   (a) ₹ 40 (b) ₹ 25
   (c) ₹ 60 (d) ₹ 48
5. 

   Priya gave ₹ 60 to buy this toy. How much will she get back?
   (a) ₹ 30 (b) ₹ 50
   (c) ₹ 48 (d) ₹ 45
6. One toy costs ₹ 40. How many toys can Rajesh buy for ₹ 120?
   (a) 2 (b) 3
   (c) 7 (d) 5
7. If one pencil costs ₹ 5, how much does Ruchi need to buy 5 pencils?
   (a) ₹ 15 (b) ₹ 35
   (c) ₹ 45 (d) ₹ 25
8. One doll costs ₹ 200. How many dolls can Priya buy for ₹ 1000?
   (a) 7 (b) 8
   (c) 5 (d) 4
9. One toy costs ₹ 150. How many toys can Gopi buy for ₹ 1500?
   (a) 15 (b) 10
   (c) 25 (d) 18
10. 

    Rani gave ₹ 100 to buy this toy. How much will she get back?
    (a) ₹ 100 (b) ₹ 114
    (c) ₹ 140 (d) ₹ 60
11. 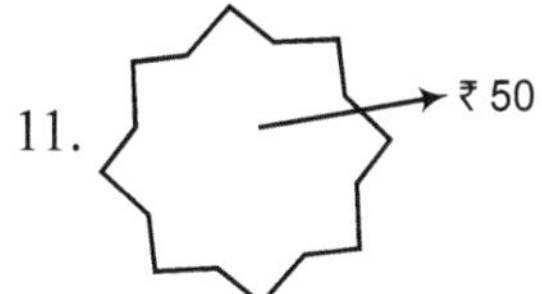

    Kisan gave ₹ 500 to buy this toy. How much will he get back?
    (a) ₹ 450 (b) ₹ 350
    (c) ₹ 150 (d) ₹ 400
12. If one pen costs ₹ 5, how much does Rajesh need to pay for 10 pens?
    (a) ₹ 45 (b) ₹ 50
    (c) ₹ 55 (d) ₹ 60
13. ₹ 2 = _______.
    (a) Four 25 Paise coins
    (b) Five 50 Paise coins
    (c) Four 50 Paise coins
    (d) Nine 10 Paise coins
14. One chocolate costs ₹ 50. How many chocolates can Mohini buy for ₹ 250?
    (a) 3 (b) 4
    (c) 6 (d) 5

15. The sum of which pair is less than ₹ 80?
(a) ₹ 50, ₹ 30 (b) ₹ 30 , ₹ 30
(c) ₹ 100, ₹ 10 (d) ₹ 80, ₹ 60

16. ₹ 4 is equal to _______.
(a) Five 50 Paise coins
(b) Four 25 Paise coins
(c) Ten 10 Paise coins
(d) Eight 50 Paise coins

17. 

How much money is enough to buy this Gulab Jamun?
(a) ₹ 15 (b) ₹ 8
(c) ₹ 20 (d) ₹ 30

18. 

How much money is enough to buy this sweater?
(a) ₹ 800 (b) ₹ 450
(c) ₹ 750 (d) ₹ 200

19. 

Priya wants to buy this can. She has ₹ 80. How much more does she need?
(a) ₹ 20 (b) ₹ 80
(c) ₹ 170 (d) ₹ 120

20. ₹ 10 is equal to _______.
(a) Four 50 Paise coins
(b) Five 50 Paise coins
(c) Ten 1 rupees coins
(d) Four 10 Paise coins

21. Which fruit has minimum cost?

(a) 

(b) 

(c) 

(d) 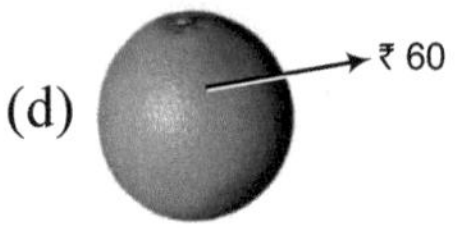

22. If one notebook costs ₹ 32, how much does Rani have to pay for 5 notebooks?
(a) ₹ 150 (b) ₹ 160
(c) ₹ 180 (d) ₹ 190

23. ₹ 5 = _______.
(a) Four 50 Paise coins and eight 25 Paise coins
(b) Eight 25 Paise coins and eight 50 Paise coins
(c) Four 25 Paise coins and eight 50 Paise coins
(d) None of these

24. The sum of which pair is smaller than ₹ 50?
(a) ₹ 50, ₹ 30 (b) ₹ 50
(c) ₹ 30, ₹ 40 (d) ₹ 20, ₹ 25

25. One ice cream costs ₹ 35. How many ice creams can Rohini buy for ₹ 70?
(a) 2 (b) 5
(c) 3 (d) 7

26. The coin which is not available is _______.
(a) ₹ 2 (b) ₹ 1
(c) ₹ 10 (d) ₹ 4

27. The coin which is available is _______.
(a) ₹ 10 (b) ₹ 20

(c) ₹ 15 (d) ₹ 40

28. One toy car costs ₹ 500. How many toy cars can Rakesh buy for ₹ 3000?
(a) 5 (b) 8
(c) 7 (d) 6

29. One teddy bear costs ₹ 40. How many teddy bears can Mohini buy for 400?
(a) 10 (b) 20
(c) 100 (d) 3

30. ₹ 2.50 – ₹ 2.00 = _______.
(a) ₹ 2 (b) 50 paise
(c) ₹ 20 (d) 20 paise

31. Rohan wants to exchange his ₹ 10 with some coins. Which of the following coins can he take?
(a) (2) (2) (5) (1)
(b) (5) (2) (1)
(c) (2) (2) (2) (2) (1)
(d) (1) (1) (5) (2)

32. If cost of one book is ₹ 30. How much money does Geeta need to pay for 2 such books?
(a) ₹ 40 (b) ₹ 50
(c) ₹ 60 (d) ₹ 80

33. How many 10-rupee notes make ₹ 100?
(a) 6 (b) 8
(c) 10 (d) 12

34. Aman has ₹ 50 with him. He gives ₹ 10 to Monu and ₹ 20 to Banti. How much money is left with Aman now?
(a) ₹ 10 (b) ₹ 15
(c) ₹ 20 (d) ₹ 30

35. If Mantu has ₹ 20, then he cannot buy which of the following :

(a) 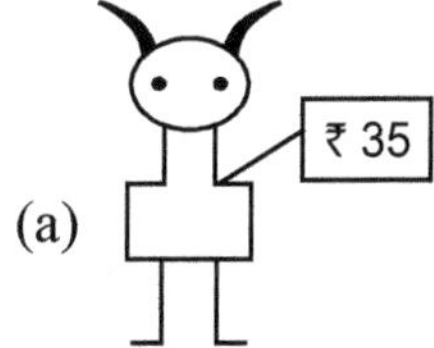

(b) 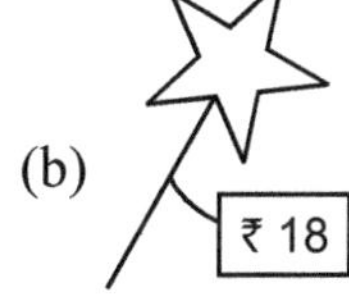

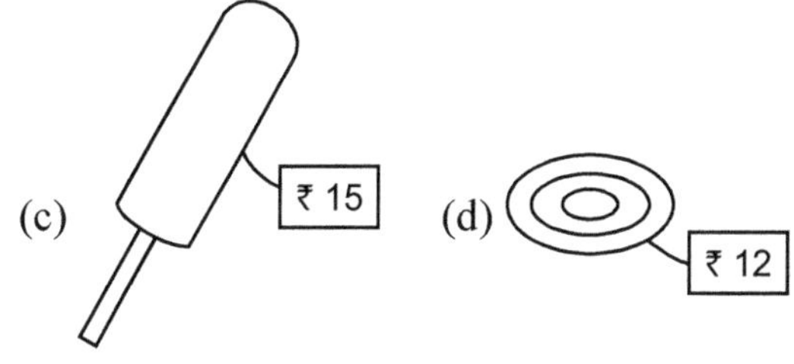

36. How many 5-rupee notes make ₹ 80?
(a) 12 (b) 14
(c) 16 (d) 20

37. Mohan gave ₹ 50 to buy this toy. How much money will he get back?

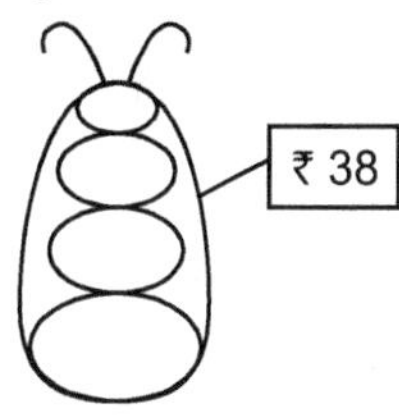

(a) ₹ 10 (b) ₹ 12
(c) ₹ 14 (d) ₹ 16

38. One toy costs ₹ 20. What is the maximum number of toys Minu can buy for ₹ 70?
(a) 2 (b) 3
(c) 4 (d) 5

Direction (39–44): Look at the price of each article and answer the following questions:

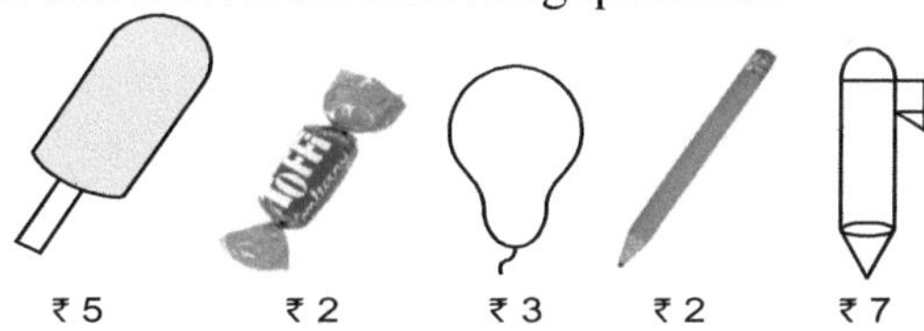

39. How much do you have to pay to buy 2 pencils and one balloon?
(a) ₹ 7 (b) ₹ 8
(c) ₹ 10 (d) ₹ 6

40. How much do you have to pay to buy three toffees and two ice-creams?
(a) ₹ 12 (b) ₹ 16
(c) ₹ 14 (d) ₹ 20

41. What is the cost of 2 pens and 3 balloons?
(a) ₹ 20 (b) ₹ 24
(c) ₹ 16 (d) ₹ 23

42. What is the total cost for three ice-creams and 4 pencils?
(a) ₹ 20 (b) ₹ 22
(c) ₹ 23 (d) ₹ 24

43. What is the total cost of 5 balloons and 6 pencils?
(a) ₹ 28 (b) ₹ 24
(c) ₹ 27 (d) ₹ 30

44. What is the cost of 5 toffees and 2 pens?
(a) ₹ 24 (b) ₹ 28
(c) ₹ 22 (d) ₹ 30

Darken Your Choice with HB Pencil

1.	ⓐ	ⓑ	ⓒ	ⓓ	10.	ⓐ	ⓑ	ⓒ	ⓓ	19.	ⓐ	ⓑ	ⓒ	ⓓ	28.	ⓐ	ⓑ	ⓒ	ⓓ	37.	ⓐ	ⓑ	ⓒ	ⓓ
2.	ⓐ	ⓑ	ⓒ	ⓓ	11.	ⓐ	ⓑ	ⓒ	ⓓ	20.	ⓐ	ⓑ	ⓒ	ⓓ	29.	ⓐ	ⓑ	ⓒ	ⓓ	38.	ⓐ	ⓑ	ⓒ	ⓓ
3.	ⓐ	ⓑ	ⓒ	ⓓ	12.	ⓐ	ⓑ	ⓒ	ⓓ	21.	ⓐ	ⓑ	ⓒ	ⓓ	30.	ⓐ	ⓑ	ⓒ	ⓓ	39.	ⓐ	ⓑ	ⓒ	ⓓ
4.	ⓐ	ⓑ	ⓒ	ⓓ	13.	ⓐ	ⓑ	ⓒ	ⓓ	22.	ⓐ	ⓑ	ⓒ	ⓓ	31.	ⓐ	ⓑ	ⓒ	ⓓ	40.	ⓐ	ⓑ	ⓒ	ⓓ
5.	ⓐ	ⓑ	ⓒ	ⓓ	14.	ⓐ	ⓑ	ⓒ	ⓓ	23.	ⓐ	ⓑ	ⓒ	ⓓ	32.	ⓐ	ⓑ	ⓒ	ⓓ	41.	ⓐ	ⓑ	ⓒ	ⓓ
6.	ⓐ	ⓑ	ⓒ	ⓓ	15.	ⓐ	ⓑ	ⓒ	ⓓ	24.	ⓐ	ⓑ	ⓒ	ⓓ	33.	ⓐ	ⓑ	ⓒ	ⓓ	42.	ⓐ	ⓑ	ⓒ	ⓓ
7.	ⓐ	ⓑ	ⓒ	ⓓ	16.	ⓐ	ⓑ	ⓒ	ⓓ	25.	ⓐ	ⓑ	ⓒ	ⓓ	34.	ⓐ	ⓑ	ⓒ	ⓓ	43.	ⓐ	ⓑ	ⓒ	ⓓ
8.	ⓐ	ⓑ	ⓒ	ⓓ	17.	ⓐ	ⓑ	ⓒ	ⓓ	26.	ⓐ	ⓑ	ⓒ	ⓓ	35.	ⓐ	ⓑ	ⓒ	ⓓ	44.	ⓐ	ⓑ	ⓒ	ⓓ
9.	ⓐ	ⓑ	ⓒ	ⓓ	18.	ⓐ	ⓑ	ⓒ	ⓓ	27.	ⓐ	ⓑ	ⓒ	ⓓ	36.	ⓐ	ⓑ	ⓒ	ⓓ					

WORKBOOK

7 Geometrical Shapes

- Shapes like squares, rectangles, circles, triangles and ovals are called plane shapes.
- A square has 4 sides and 4 corners. All its sides have the same length.

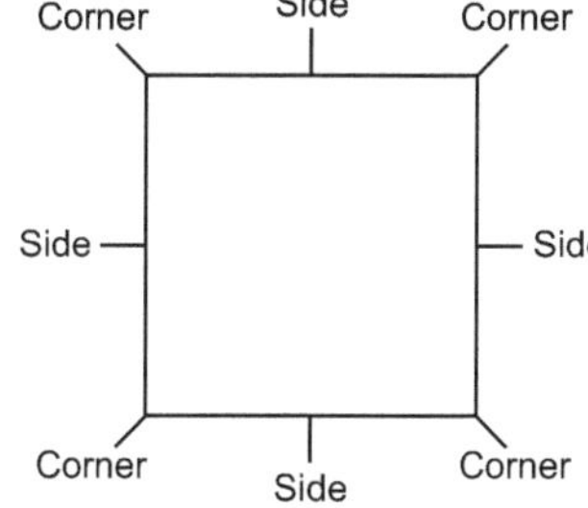

- Rectangle also has 4 sides and 4 corners. Its opposite sides have the same length.

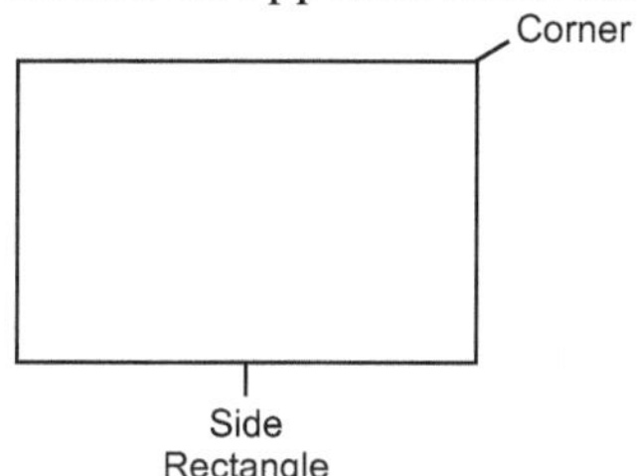

Rectangle

- A triangle has 3 sides and 3 corners. The three sides of the triangle may or may not be of the same length.

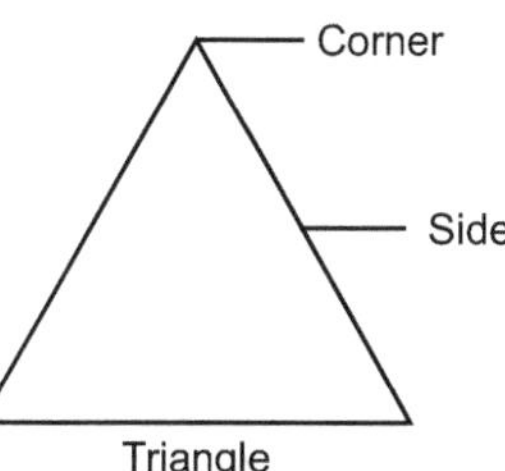

Triangle

- Circle has no sides or corners. It has radius, diameter and circumference.

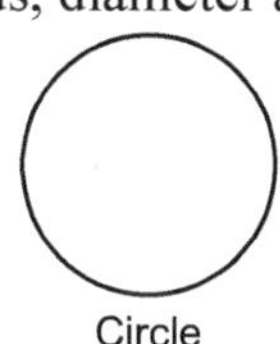
Circle

- An oval also has no sides or corners.

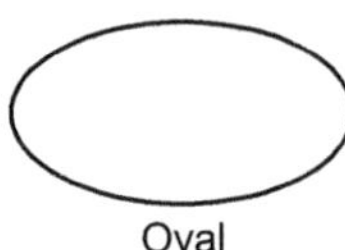

Oval

- Shapes like cube, cuboid, cylinder, sphere and cone are called solid shapes.
- Cube has 6 equal flat surfaces.

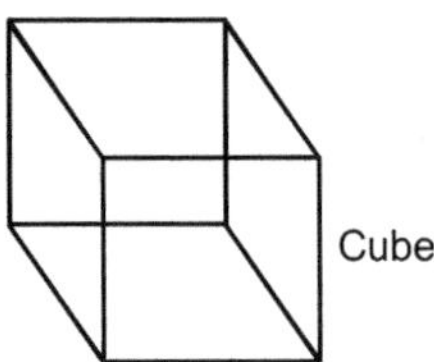

- Cuboid has 6 flat surfaces.

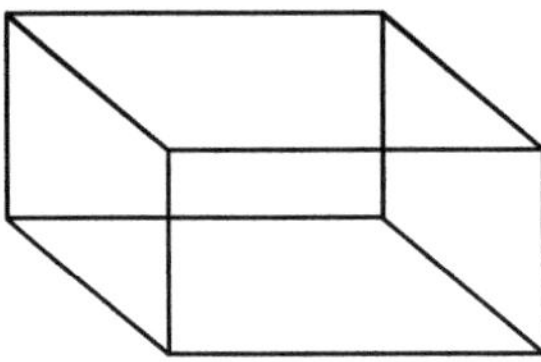

- Cylinder has 2 flat faces and 1 curved face.

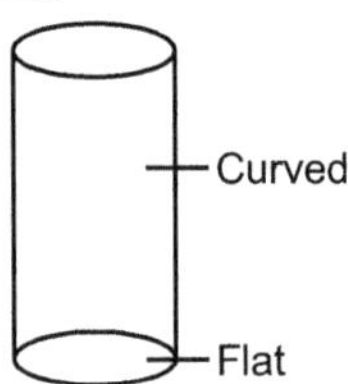

- Sphere has only 1 curved face.

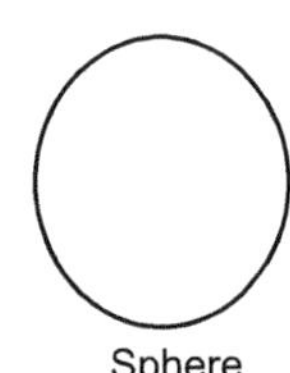

Sphere

- Cone has one curved face and one flat face.

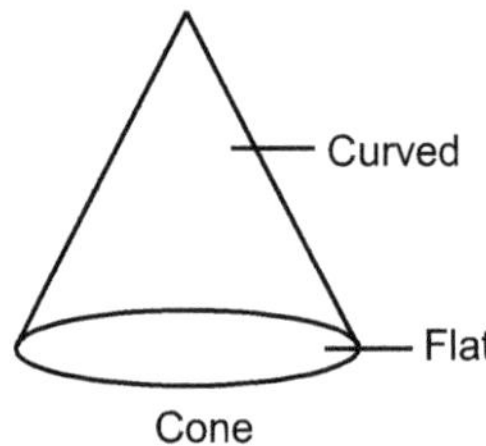

Cone

Multiple Choice Questions

1. Which shape is not shown here?

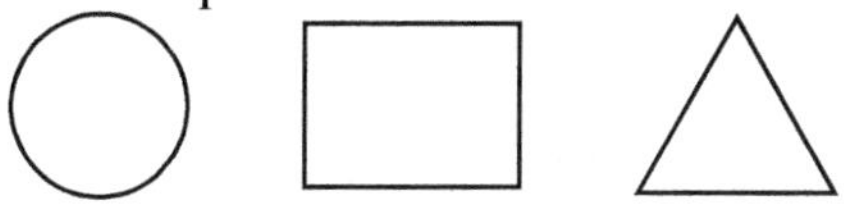

(a) Triangle (b) Rectangle
(c) Square (d) Circle

2. How many triangles are there in the box?

(a) 4 (b) 6
(c) 8 (d) 5

3. How many circles are shown here?

(a) 5 (b) 6
(c) 7 (d) 8

4. Which of the following shapes is an oval?

(a) 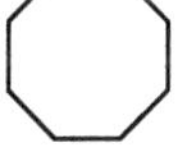 (b) 
(c)  (d)

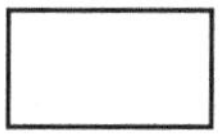

5. Name the shape which is shaded below?

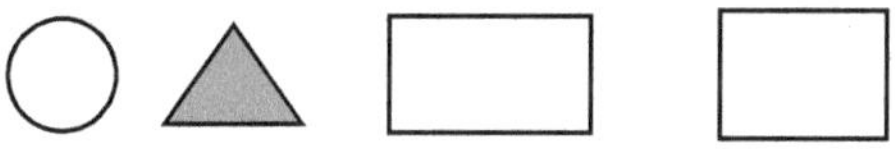

(a) Circle (b) Square
(c) Rectangle (d) Triangle

6. Name the shape which is shaded below?

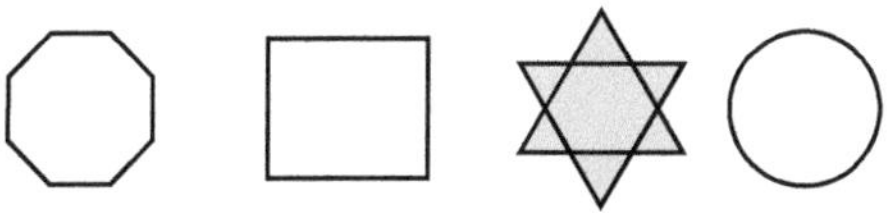

(a) Octagon (b) Square
(c) Star (d) Circle

7. Circle can be traced using ______
(a) Cube
(b) Cylinder
(c) Cuboid
(d) Sphere

8. How many triangles are shown here?

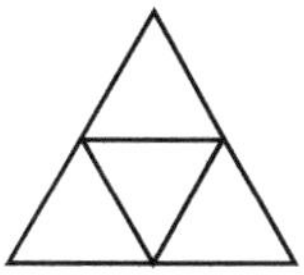

(a) 4 (b) 5
(c) 3 (d) 2

9. Which shape is an octagon?

(a)  (b) 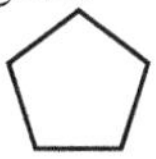
(c) 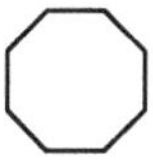 (d)

10. Pencil box is _______.
(a) Cylinder (b) Cuboid
(c) Cone (d) Sphere

11. The figure is made up of how many circles?

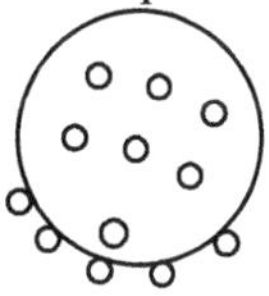

(a) 10 (b) 11
(c) 12 (d) 13

12. How many octagons are there in the box?

(a) 6 (b) 2
(c) 3 (d) 5

13. Which of the following looks like a cone?

(a)  – Icecream (b) – Ball

(c) – Dice (d) – Pipe

14. The name of shape of the shaded part is ________.

(a) Octogon (b) Rectangle
(c) Cone (d) Triangle

15. The figure is made up of how many squares?

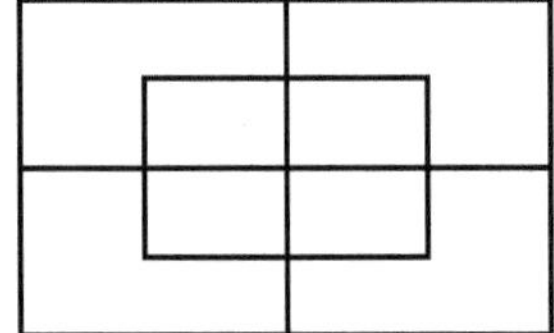

(a) 2 (b) 4
(c) 6 (d) None of these

16. A triangle is a closed planar shape with _____.
(a) 2 sides (b) 4 sides
(c) 3 sides (d) 5 sides

17. A closed planar shape with 5 sides is called a ________.
(a) Pentagon (b) Hexagon
(c) Square (d) Heptagon

18. Number of line segments used in the figure of a cuboid is ________.
(a) 6 (b) 8
(c) 1 (d) None of these

19. Name the shape which is shaded below?

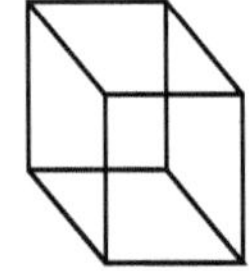 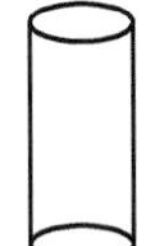 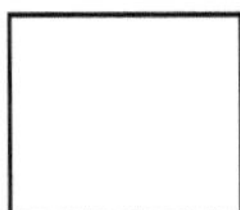 

(a) Cylinder
(b) Square
(c) Octagon
(d) Half circle

20. How many half circles are there in the box?

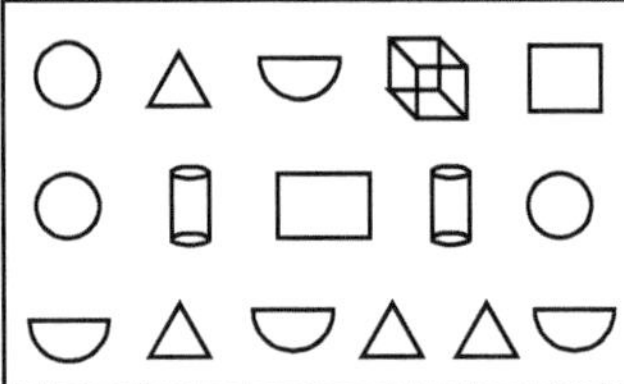

(a) 4 (b) 5
(c) 3 (d) 6

21. Which figure is not shown here?

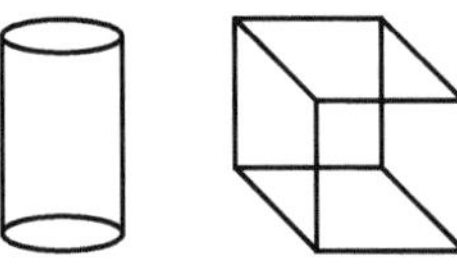 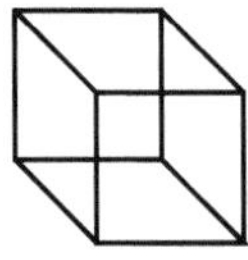 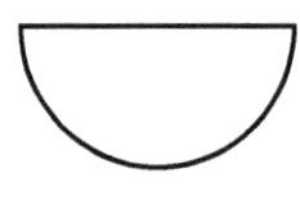

(a) Half circle (b) Cone
(c) Cube (d) Cylinder

22. How many circles are there in the figure?

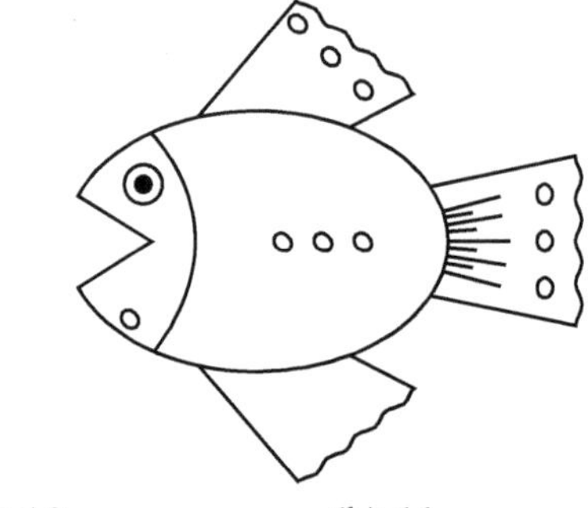

(a) 10 (b) 11
(c) 12 (d) 15

23. The shape of the shaded part is ________.

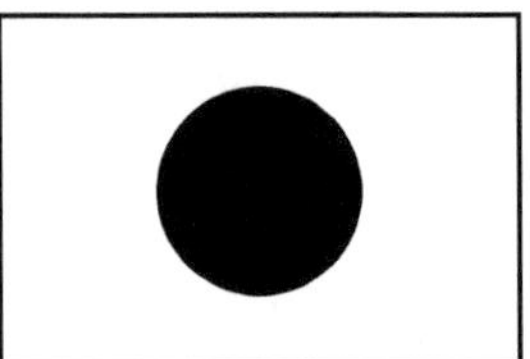

(a) Square (b) Cuboid
(c) Cylinder (d) Circle

24. Which of the following looks like a cuboid?

(a) 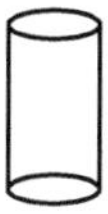 (b)

(c)  (d)

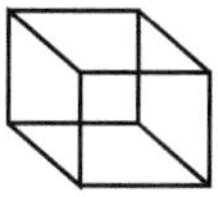

25. The instrument used to measure an angle is a _______.

(a) Ruler (b) Protractor
(c) Divider (d) Compasses

26. Path described by any moving point is classified as _______.

(a) Ordinate ray (b) Rays
(c) Line segment (d) Line

27. Ravi has 5 groups of shapes.

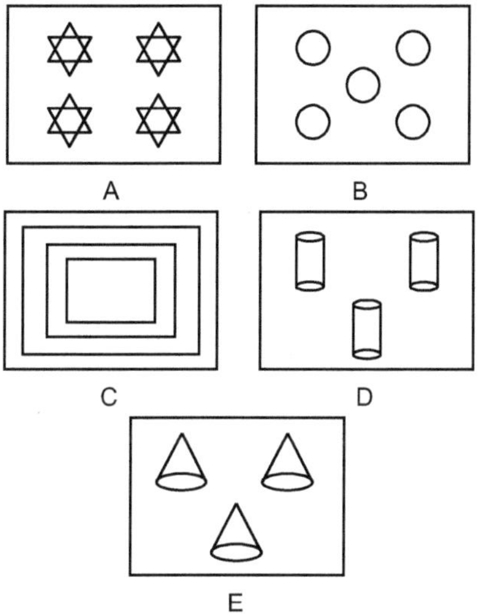

A B C D E

In which group will he put a cone?

(a) E (b) A
(c) D (d) C

28. An oval has _______ sides.

(a) 0 (b) 1
(c) 2 (d) 3

29. How many square faces does a cube have?

(a) 4 (b) 5
(c) 8 (d) 6

30. Which 2D shape has 6 sides?

(a) Pentagon (b) Octagon
(c) Hexagon (d) Triangle

31. Flat face of a cube is a _______.

(a) Oval (b) Square
(c) Rectangle (d) Triangle

32. A cube has _______ flat faces.

(a) 2 (b) 6
(c) 4 (d) 8

33. Given line is _______.

(a) Slant (b) Curved
(c) Straight (d) None of these

34. A square has _______ diagonals.

(a) 2 (b) 3
(c) 4 (d) 6

35. A rectangle has _______ corners.

(a) 4 (b) 6
(c) 2 (d) 0

36. A line has _______ end points.

(a) 1 (b) 2
(c) No (d) 5

37. A square has _______ equal sides.

(a) 3 (b) 2
(c) 4 (d) 6

38. A _______ is the smallest geometrical shape.

(a) Point (b) Line
(c) (a) and (b) (d) Triangle

39. A sphere has _______ curved face.

(a) 4 (b) 3
(c) 2 (d) 1

40. A notebook is shaped like a _______

(a) Square (b) Cuboid
(c) Rectangle (d) Triangle

41. Name of the shape of shaded part is ________.

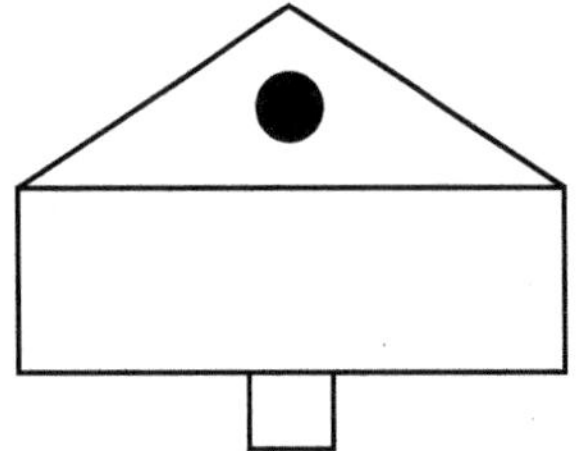

(a) Square (b) Circle
(c) Triangle (d) Rectangle

42. The difference between number of circles and triangles is ________

(a) 2 (b) 3
(c) 4 (d) 5

43. Which of the following is a triangle?

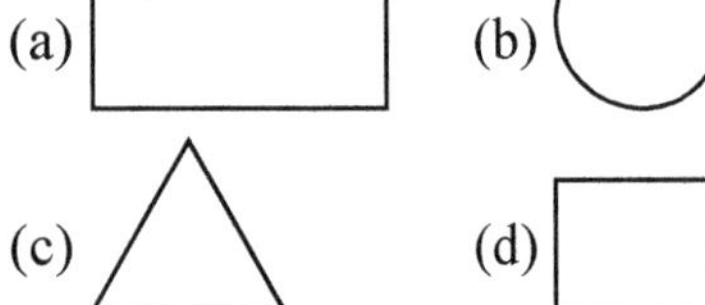

44. How many squares are there in the given figure?

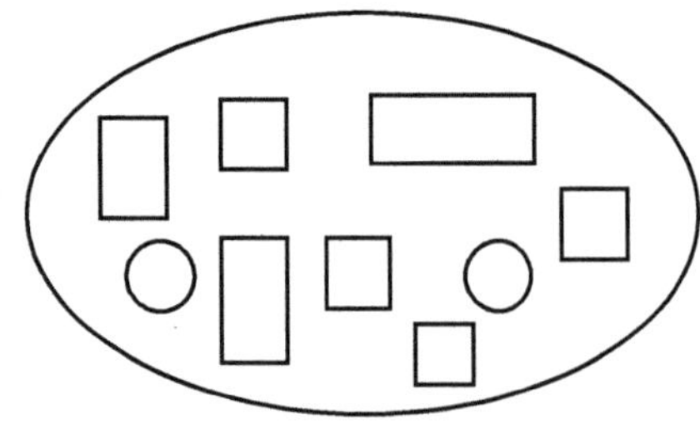

(a) 2 (b) 3
(c) 4 (d) 5

45. Which of the following looks like a cylinder?

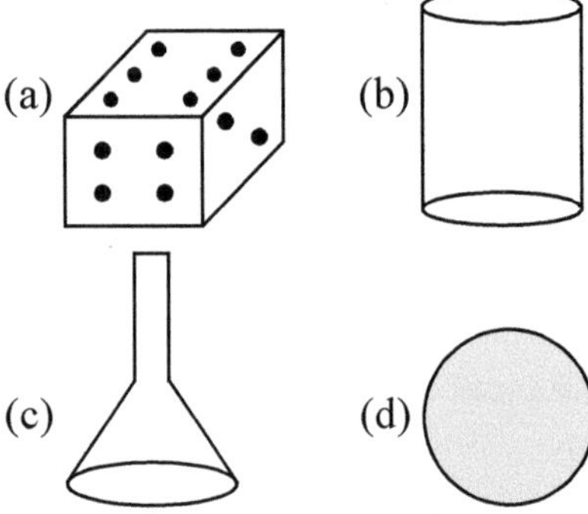

46. Which of the following figures is not shown here?

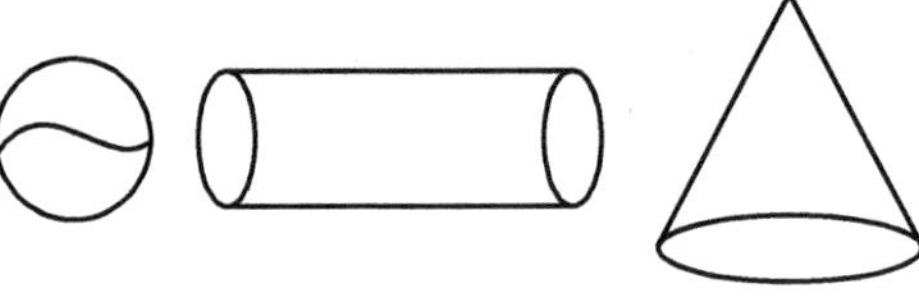

(a) Cone (b) Cube
(c) Sphere (d) Cylinder

47. Name the shape which is shaded?

(a) Circle (b) Square
(c) Rectangle (d) Triangle

48. Which shape is not shown here?

 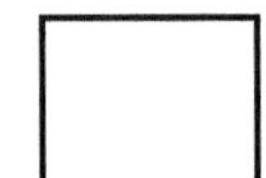 

(a) Triangle (b) Square
(c) Circle (d) Rectangle

49. Which shapes make up this arrow?

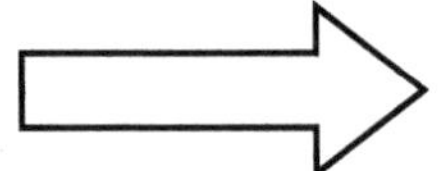

(a) Triangle, Rectangle
(b) Oval, Triangle
(c) Rectangle, Circle
(d) Circle, Oval

50. Which of the following looks like a cube?

(a) 

(b) 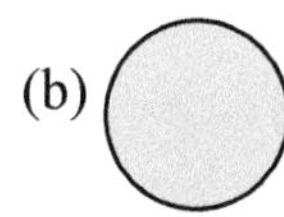

(c) 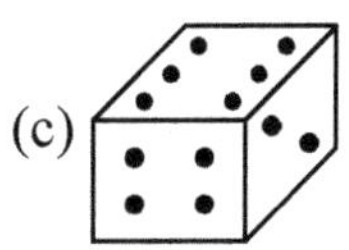

(d) 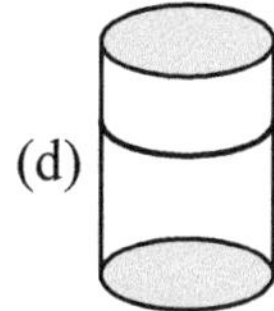

51.How many curved lines are there in a square?

(a) 0 (b) 3

(c) 4 (d) 5

52. Aman has four groups of shapes.

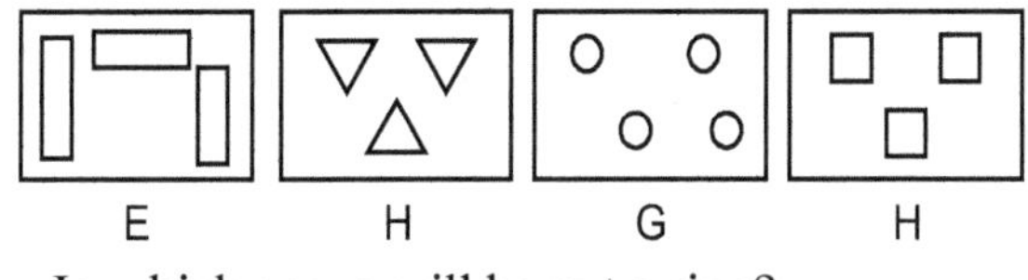

In which group will he put a ring?

(a) E (b) F

(c) G (d) H

53. What is the total number of triangles and circles in the boxes?

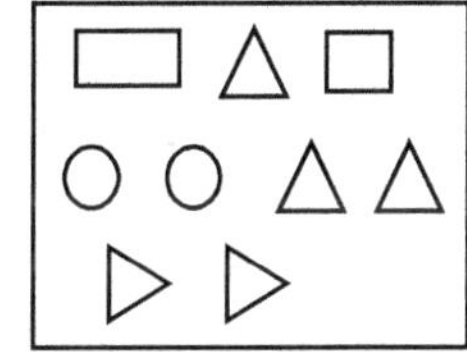
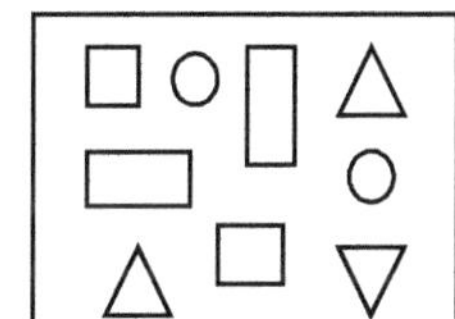

(a) 10 (b) 11

(c) 12 (d) 14

54. What is the total number of squares and triangles in the boxes?

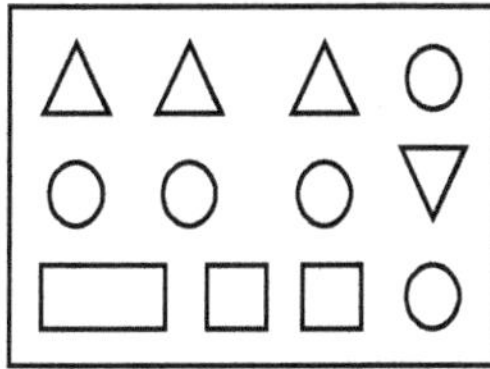
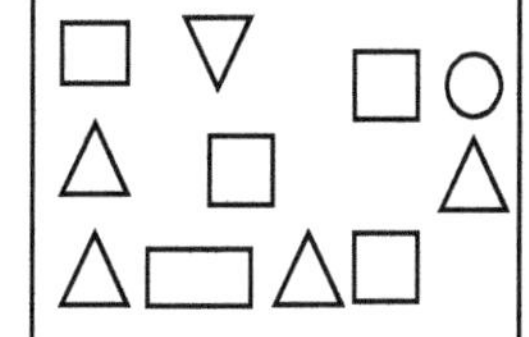

(a) 13 (b) 14

(c) 15 (d) 16

55. Which of the following is incorrectly matched?

(a) — Rectangle

(b) — Triangle

(c) — Pentagon

(d) — Circle

56. Which of the following is correctly matched?

(a) 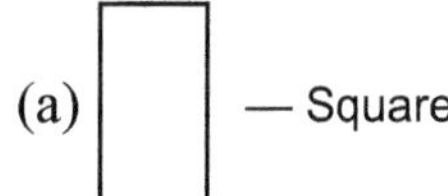

(b) 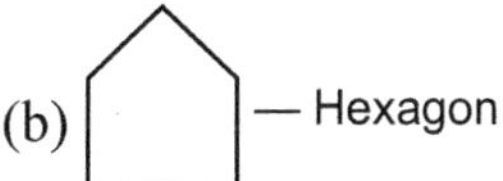

(c) 

(d) 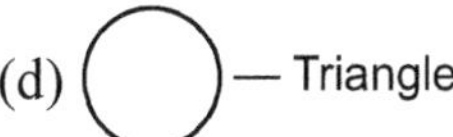

57. How many circles are there in the given figure?

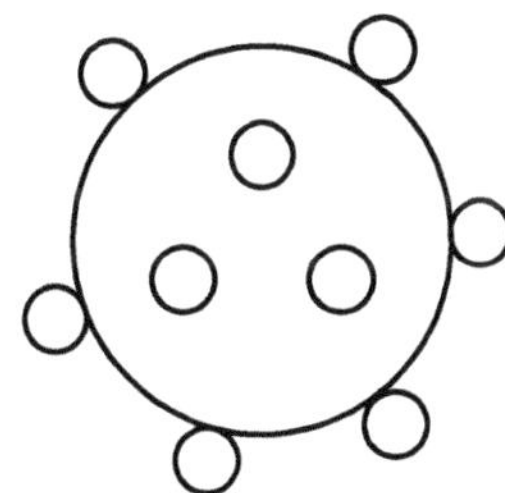

(a) 8 (b) 9

(c) 10 (d) 12

58. Which of the following shapes is shaded?

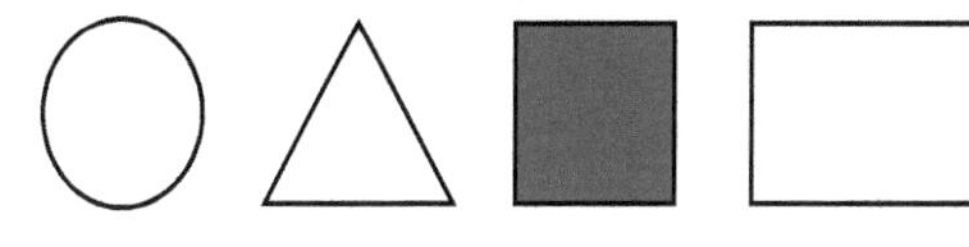

(a) Rectangle b) Square

(c) Circle (d) Triangle

59. How many rectangles and circles are there in the given figure?

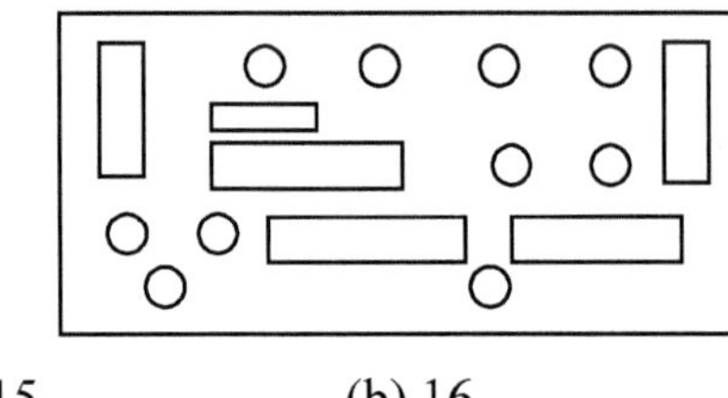

(a) 15 (b) 16

(c) 17 (d) 18

60. Which of the following shapes is a hexagon?

(a) 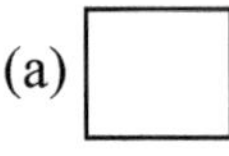

(b) 

(c) 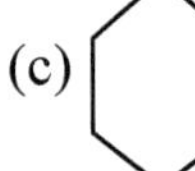

(d) 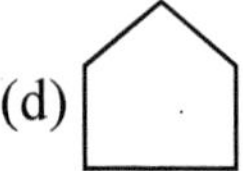

Darken Your Choice with HB Pencil

1.	ⓐ	ⓑ	ⓒ	ⓓ	13.	ⓐ	ⓑ	ⓒ	ⓓ	25.	ⓐ	ⓑ	ⓒ	ⓓ	37.	ⓐ	ⓑ	ⓒ	ⓓ	49.	ⓐ	ⓑ	ⓒ	ⓓ
2.	ⓐ	ⓑ	ⓒ	ⓓ	14.	ⓐ	ⓑ	ⓒ	ⓓ	26.	ⓐ	ⓑ	ⓒ	ⓓ	38.	ⓐ	ⓑ	ⓒ	ⓓ	50.	ⓐ	ⓑ	ⓒ	ⓓ
3.	ⓐ	ⓑ	ⓒ	ⓓ	15.	ⓐ	ⓑ	ⓒ	ⓓ	27.	ⓐ	ⓑ	ⓒ	ⓓ	39.	ⓐ	ⓑ	ⓒ	ⓓ	51.	ⓐ	ⓑ	ⓒ	ⓓ
4.	ⓐ	ⓑ	ⓒ	ⓓ	16.	ⓐ	ⓑ	ⓒ	ⓓ	28.	ⓐ	ⓑ	ⓒ	ⓓ	40.	ⓐ	ⓑ	ⓒ	ⓓ	52.	ⓐ	ⓑ	ⓒ	ⓓ
5.	ⓐ	ⓑ	ⓒ	ⓓ	17.	ⓐ	ⓑ	ⓒ	ⓓ	29.	ⓐ	ⓑ	ⓒ	ⓓ	41.	ⓐ	ⓑ	ⓒ	ⓓ	53.	ⓐ	ⓑ	ⓒ	ⓓ
6.	ⓐ	ⓑ	ⓒ	ⓓ	18.	ⓐ	ⓑ	ⓒ	ⓓ	30.	ⓐ	ⓑ	ⓒ	ⓓ	42.	ⓐ	ⓑ	ⓒ	ⓓ	54.	ⓐ	ⓑ	ⓒ	ⓓ
7.	ⓐ	ⓑ	ⓒ	ⓓ	19.	ⓐ	ⓑ	ⓒ	ⓓ	31.	ⓐ	ⓑ	ⓒ	ⓓ	43.	ⓐ	ⓑ	ⓒ	ⓓ	55.	ⓐ	ⓑ	ⓒ	ⓓ
8.	ⓐ	ⓑ	ⓒ	ⓓ	20.	ⓐ	ⓑ	ⓒ	ⓓ	32.	ⓐ	ⓑ	ⓒ	ⓓ	44.	ⓐ	ⓑ	ⓒ	ⓓ	56.	ⓐ	ⓑ	ⓒ	ⓓ
9.	ⓐ	ⓑ	ⓒ	ⓓ	21.	ⓐ	ⓑ	ⓒ	ⓓ	33.	ⓐ	ⓑ	ⓒ	ⓓ	45.	ⓐ	ⓑ	ⓒ	ⓓ	57.	ⓐ	ⓑ	ⓒ	ⓓ
10.	ⓐ	ⓑ	ⓒ	ⓓ	22.	ⓐ	ⓑ	ⓒ	ⓓ	34.	ⓐ	ⓑ	ⓒ	ⓓ	46.	ⓐ	ⓑ	ⓒ	ⓓ	58.	ⓐ	ⓑ	ⓒ	ⓓ
11.	ⓐ	ⓑ	ⓒ	ⓓ	23.	ⓐ	ⓑ	ⓒ	ⓓ	35.	ⓐ	ⓑ	ⓒ	ⓓ	47.	ⓐ	ⓑ	ⓒ	ⓓ	59.	ⓐ	ⓑ	ⓒ	ⓓ
12.	ⓐ	ⓑ	ⓒ	ⓓ	24.	ⓐ	ⓑ	ⓒ	ⓓ	36.	ⓐ	ⓑ	ⓒ	ⓓ	48.	ⓐ	ⓑ	ⓒ	ⓓ	60.	ⓐ	ⓑ	ⓒ	ⓓ

WORKBOOK

Logical Reasoning

PATTERN

- Pattern is a repeated sequence of letters, numbers and shapes, which has a particular logical design.
- Pattern can be classified as identification of missing number in a number series or missing letter in a letter series, pattern or identification of missing part in a figure.

Example 1 : Complete the pattern by choosing the next figure?

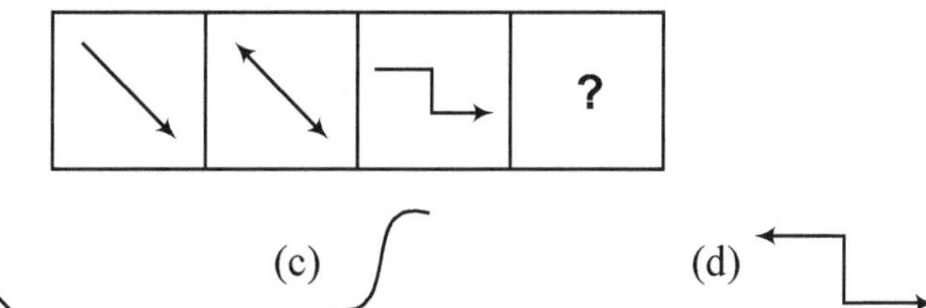

Ans. (d)

Example 2 : Find the next figures in the figure pattern.

(a) (b) (c) (d)

Ans. (b)

Example 3 : Which number comes next in the given number pattern?

(a) 40 (b) 45 (c) 50 (d) 55

Ans. (a)

10 15 20 25 30 35 40

+5 +5 +5 +5 +5 +5

ODD ONE OUT

- Odd one out is to point out the component which does not fit in a group. For example, a bird among a group of lions is odd.
- In these types of questions we need to identify an odd object, a shape, or a number.

Example 1 : Find the odd one out.

(a)  (b)  (c) 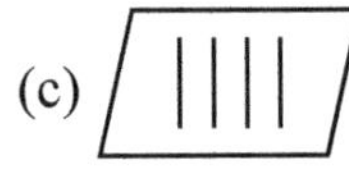 (d) 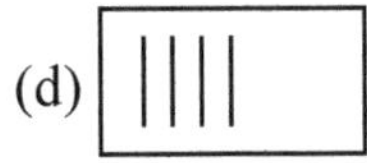

Ans. (b)

Example 2 : Select the odd one out.

(a) 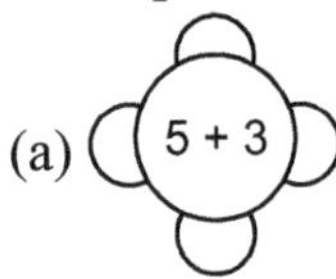

(b) 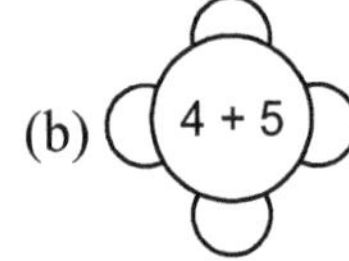

(c) 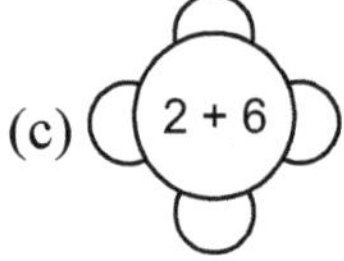

(d) 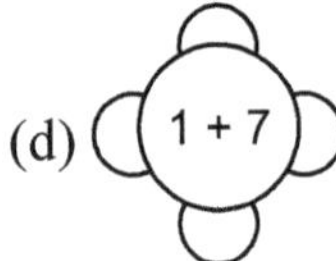

Ans. (b) As in other three figures, sum = 8

Example 3 : Choose the odd one out.

20, 24, 28, 32, 36, 38, 44

(a) 36 (b) 38 (c) 28 (d) 44

Ans. (b)

MEASURING UNITS

- Measurement is related to counting or measuring an object. The parameters of measurement are length, weight, volume, time and money.
- Length of an object is measured in meter or centimeter.

  1 meter (m) = 100 centimeters (cm)

- Mass of an object is measured in kilogram (kg) or gram (gm).

  1 kg = 1000 gm

- Volume is the amount of liquid which is contained in a particular pot.

  For example, Milk, Oil, Water, Juice in a container.

- Volume is measured in litre (*l*) or milliliter (*ml*)

  1 *l* = 100 *ml*

- We use a clock or watch to check the time.

  Time is measured in hours, minutes, and seconds.

  1 hour = 60 minutes

  1 minute = 60 seconds

  1 day = 24 hours

1 week = 7 days
1 year = 12 months

- Money is represented by Rupee in India.

1 rupee = 100 paise

- Symbol of rupee = ₹

Example 1 : In the given figure, what is the length of pencil?

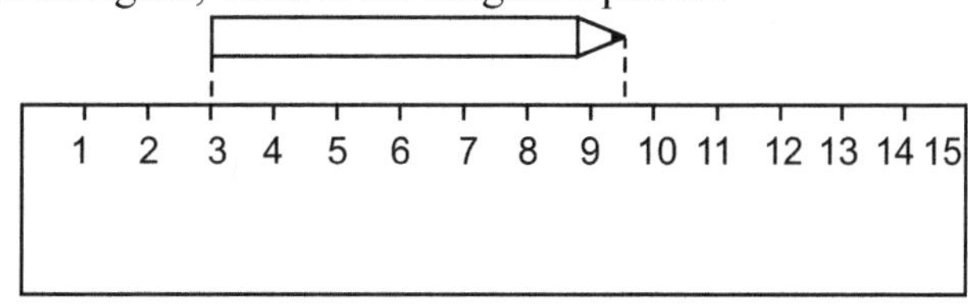

(a) 6 cm (b) 6.5 cm (c) 7 cm (d) 7.5 cm

Ans. (b) 9.5 – 3 = 6.5 cm

Example 2 : How many centimeters are there in 4 meters?

(a) 200 cm (b) 300 cm (c) 400 cm (d) 500 cm

Ans. (c) 1 m = 100 cm
4 m = 4 × 100 = 400 cm

Example 3 : How many days are there in 5 weeks?

(a) 15 (b) 20 (c) 25 (d) 35

Ans. (d) 1 week = 7 days
5 weeks = 5 × 7 = 35 days

Example 4 : How many grams are there in 2 kg of sugar?

(a) 500 gm (b) 1000 gm (c) 2000 gm (d) 2500 gm

Ans. (c) 1 kg = 1000 gm
2 kg = 2 × 1000 = 2000 gm

SPATIAL UNDERSTANDING

Spatial Understanding is an organized knowledge of objects in relation to oneself in a given space. Spatial awareness also involves understanding the relationship of the objects when there is a change of position.

Example 1 : Which of the following shapes and patterns matches the given figure?

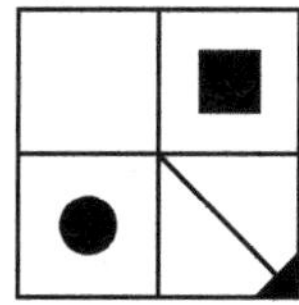

(a) 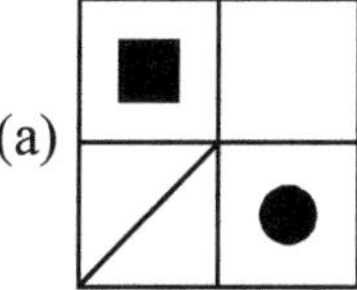 (b) 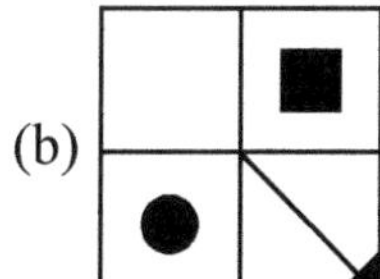 (c) 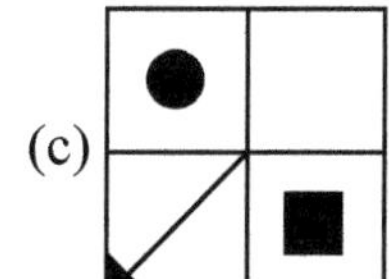 (d) 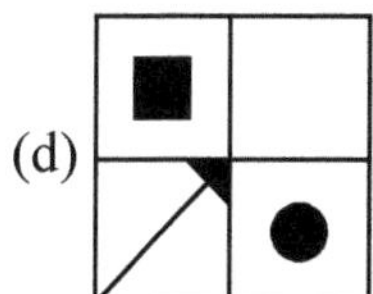

Ans. (b and c)

Example 2 : Identify the object which is under the table?

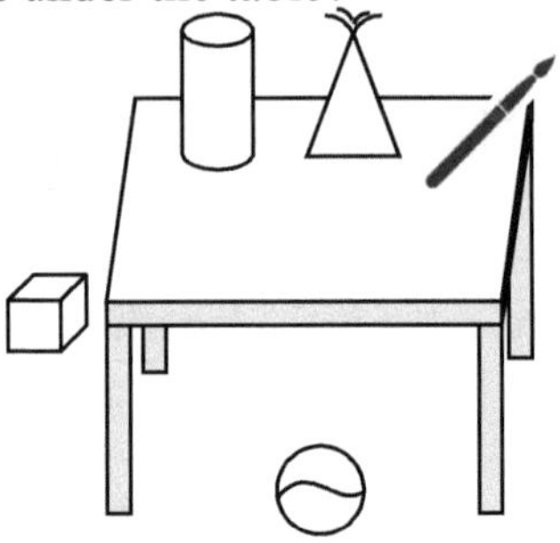

(a) 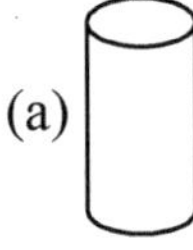 (b)  (c) 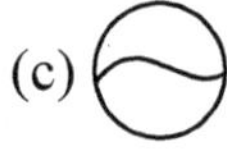 (d) 

Ans. (c)

ANALOGY

- Analogy means comparison of two things that have some relationship on the basis of their similarities.
- In these types of questions, sutudents have to find out the relation among different options.

Example 1 : Find out the relation and the missing character.

Uttarakhand : Dehradun : Bihar : ?

(a) Jaipur (b) Ranchi (c) Patna (d) Gandhinagar

Ans. (c) In this question, the state with capital is given.

Example 2 : Find the missing shape by identifying the relationship.

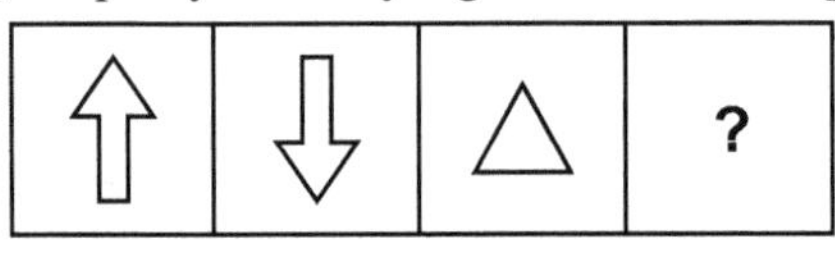

(a)  (b)  (c)  (d)

Ans. (b) First figure rotates vertically downwards.

Example 3 : If  is to  then  is to …….. ?

(a) 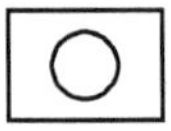 (b)  (c) 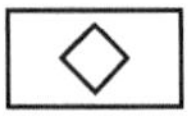 (d)

Ans. (c)

GROUPING OF FIGURES

- In grouping of figures, a set of figures or numbers are grouped on the basis of certain properties or parameters. The basic fundamental of fractioning, division and multiplication are applied while grouping of figures.

  Example 1 : There are 3 groups. In which of the following groups the numbers contain 5 as a digit?

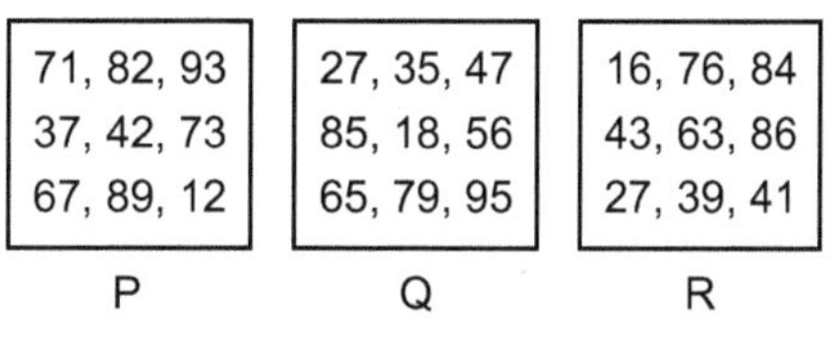

(a) P (b) Q (c) R (d) Q & R

Ans. (b) Group Q has 35, 85, 56, 65, 95, numbers which contain 5.

Example 2 : How many groups of 3 rectangles can be formed from the group of associated shapes given in the box?

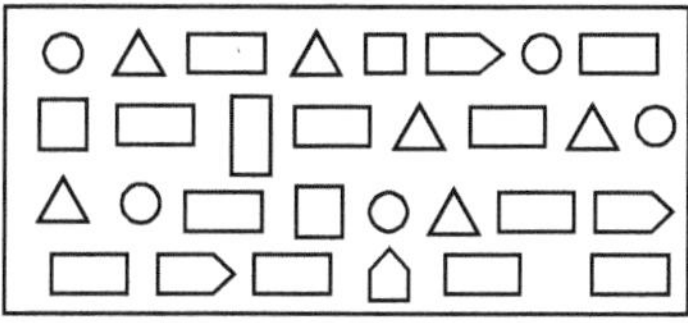

(a) 2 (b) 3 (c) 4 (d) 5

Ans. (c) There are 12 rectangles.

$12 = 3 \times 4$, so there are 4 groups of 3.

Example 3 : The shape ⌂ belongs to which of the following groups.

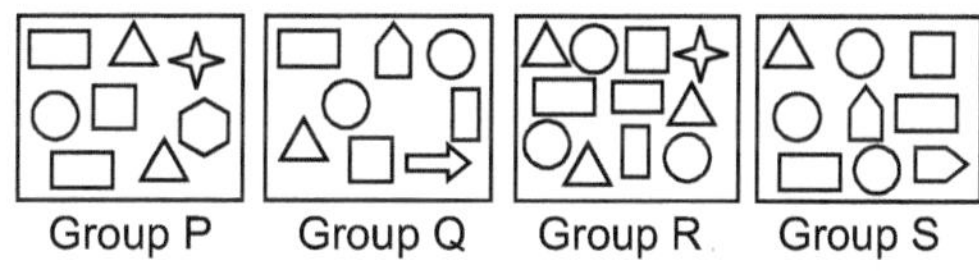

(a) P (b) Q (c) Q & R (d) Q & S

Ans. (d) The shape ⌂ is present in Q and S groups.

RANKING TEST

- Ranking is based on arrangement of different things like persons, objects or characters based on some special features in a specific order.
- In ranking test, the position or rank of an object or person is identified from left end or right end or from top or bottom.
- This test is based on the position of an object with respect to other person or object.

  Example 1 : Which letter is the fourth from left end in the given word.

MATHEMATICS

(a) A (b) E (c) H (d) T

Ans. (c) M A T H E M A T I C S

Left end → 1 2 3 4 5 6 7 8 9 10 11

H is the fourth letter from left end.

Example 2 : 6th pencil is before which of the following pencils.

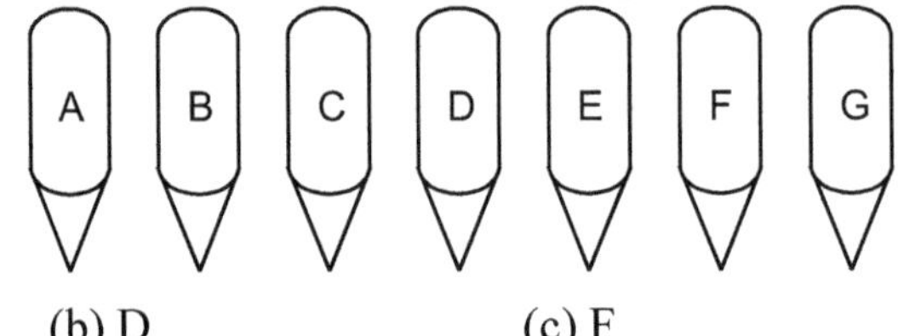

(a) C (b) D (c) F (d) G

Ans. (d) 6th pencil is F which is before G.

PROBLEMS BASED ON FIGURES

➠ In this type of questions, some figures are given. The problems are based on the given figures.

Example 1 : How many balls are outside the basket?

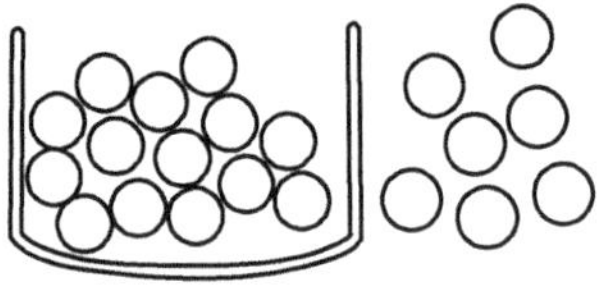

(a) 5 (b) 6 (c) 7 (d) 8

Ans. (c)

Example 2 : Which of the following is biggest in size?

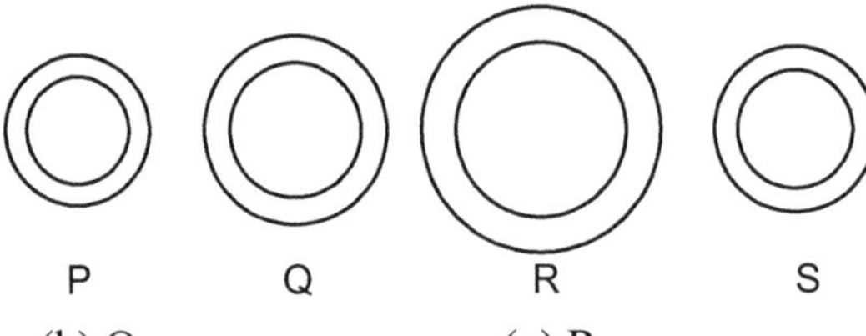

(a) P (b) Q (c) R (d) S

Ans. (c) R is the biggest in size.

Example 3 : Which of the following is same as the given figure X ?

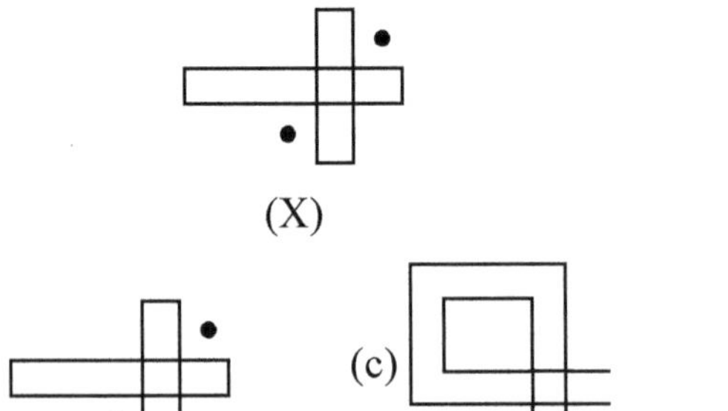

(X)

(a) (b) (c) (d)

Ans. (b)

Multiple Choice Questions

Direction (1– 6) : Find the missing number in the given patterns.

1. 2, 6, ________, 54, 162

   (a) 12 (b) 16
   (c) 18 (d) 24

2. [7 | 42 | 6]   [2 | ? | 8]

   (a) 11 (b) 16
   (c) 18 (d) 14

3. 10, 15, 20, 25, 30, ________

   (a) 32, 34 (b) 35, 37
   (c) 35, 45 (d) 35, 40

4. 16, 12, 8, ________

   (a) 3 (b) 4
   (c) 6 (d) 5

5. 72, 36, 18, ________

   (a) 7 (b) 8
   (c) 9 (d) 11

6. 2, 3, 5, 7, 11, 13, ________

   (a) 14 (b) 15
   (c) 19 (d) 17

Direction (7–11) : Observe the figures carefully and answer the following questions.

7. Who is sitting between R and T?

   (a) P (b) Q
   (c) R (d) S

8. Who is sitting on the 5th position from right?

   (a) P (b) S
   (c) T (d) U

9. Who is sitting on the sixth position from left?

   (a) U (b) V
   (c) T (d) S

10. If P and R exchange their positions, then who is sitting in the left side of S?

    (a) P (b) Q
    (c) R (d) T

11. Who is sitting on the seventh position from right?

    (a) P (b) Q
    (c) R (d) S

Direction (12–18) : Find the odd one out.

12. (a)  (b) 

    (c) 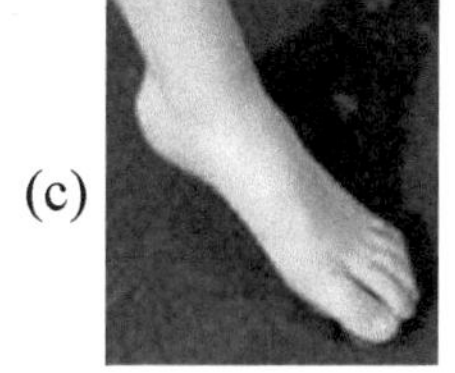 (d) 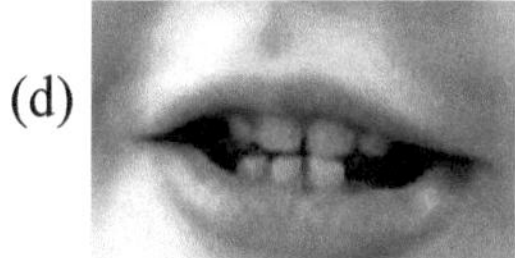

13. (a) 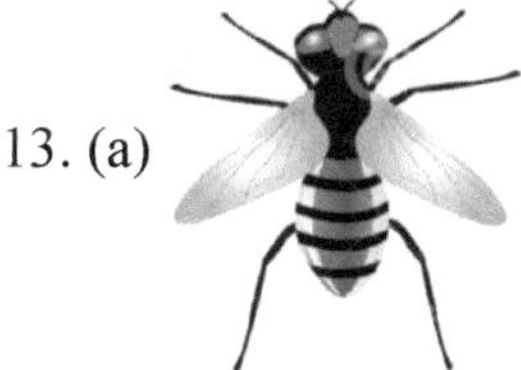 (b) 

    (c) 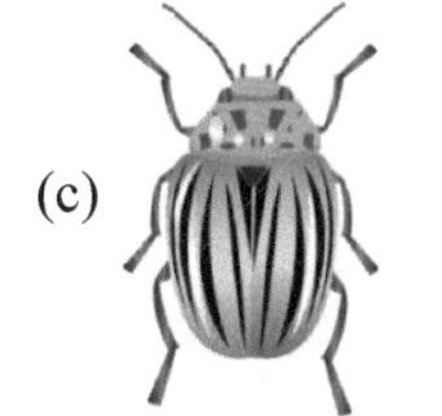 (d) 

14. (a) Cow (b) Elephant
    (c) Goat (d) Buffalo

15. (a) Rose (b) Mango
    (c) Pineapple (d) Apple

16. (a) Uttar Pradesh (b) Bihar
(c) Mumbai (d) Tamil Nadu

17. (a) Nose (b) Ear
(c) Eye (d) Hand

18. (a) Textbook (b) Book
(c) Pen (d) Novel

Direction (19–25) : Complete the following patterns by choosing the correct figure.

19. ?

(a) (b)

(c) (d)

20. ?

(a) (b)

(c) (d)

21. ?

(a) (b)

(c) (d)

22. ?

(a) (b)

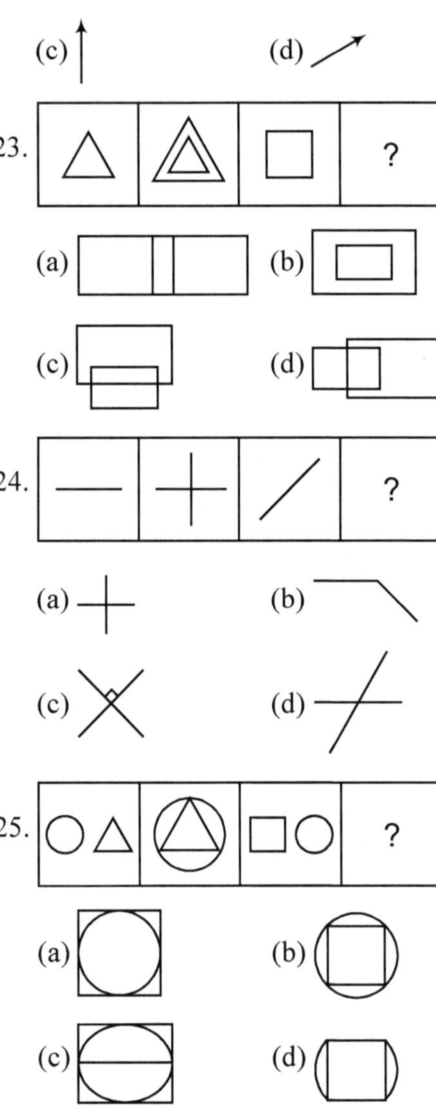

Direction (26–32) : Six persons A, B, C, D, E and F are sitting in a straight line, as shown below.

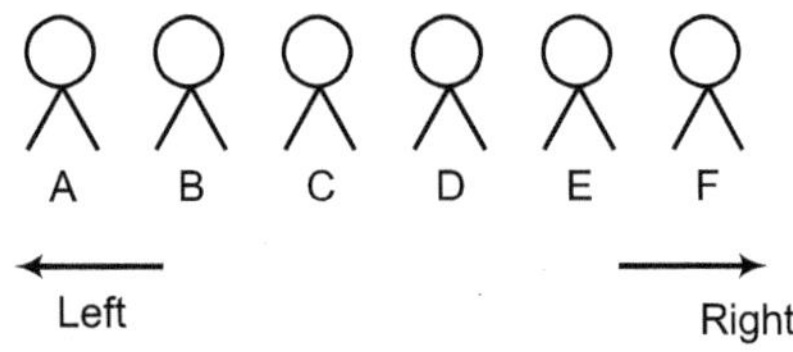

26. Who is sitting on the first position from the right?
(a) A (b) E
(c) F (d) B

27. What is the position of C from left?
(a) Fourth (b) Third
(c) Second (d) Fifth

28. Who is sitting on the immediate left of D?
(a) C (b) E
(c) B (d) F

29. What is the position of C from E?
(a) Second from left
(b) Second from right
(c) Third from left
(d) Fifth from right

30. If A and B interchange their positions, what will be the position of A from left?
(a) First (b) Fifth
(c) Second (d) Sixth

31. If E and F interchange their positions, who will be the neighbours of D?
(a) C and E (b) C and F
(c) F and B (d) E and B

32. Who is sitting on the second left position from D?
(a) A (b) B
(c) E (d) F

33. How many triangles are there in the given figure?

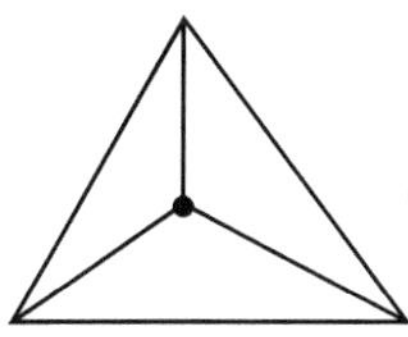

(a) 3 (b) 2
(c) 4 (d) 6

34. How many slanting lines are shown in the following figure?

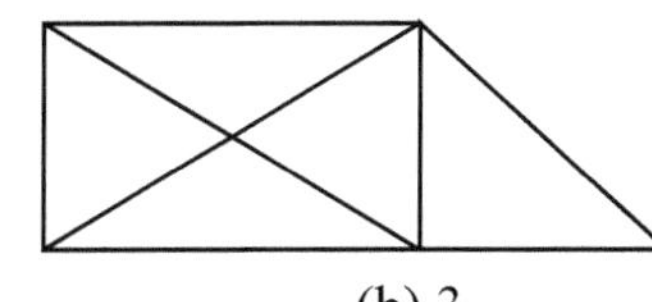

(a) 1 (b) 3
(c) 2 (d) 4

35. How many curved lines are shown in the figure below?

(a) 3 (b) 5
(c) 7 (d) 12

36. How many horizontal lines are there in the given figure?

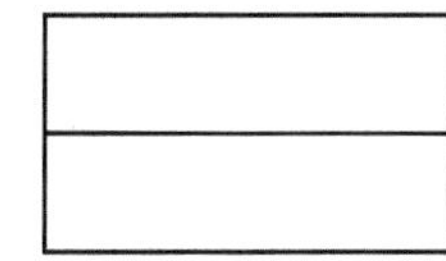

(a) 2 (b) 6
(c) 3 (d) 4

Direction (37–52) : Complete the given patterns by selecting the correct option.

37. 11, 12, 13, 14, _______
(a) 16 (b) 15
(c) 17 (d) 18

38. 21, 25, 29, _______
(a) 28 (b) 32
(c) 33 (d) 36

39. 9, 18, 27, 36, _______
(a) 38, 45 (b) 45, 56
(c) 46, 54 (d) 45, 54

40. 56, 28, 14, _______
(a) 2 (b) 6
(c) 7 (d) 9

41. 17, 14, 11, _______
(a) 8, 5 (b) 7, 6
(c) 8, 6 (d) 9, 5

42. 11, 9, 7, 5, _______
(a) 2, 3 (b) 3, 4
(c) 3, 1 (d) 3, 2

43. 2, 3, 5, 7, _______
(a) 17, 18 (b) 11, 12
(c) 11, 14 (d) 11, 13

44. 3, 6, 9, 12, ______
(a) 16 (b) 18
(c) 15 (d) 19

45. 50, 46, 42, 38, ______
(a) 36, 32 (b) 34, 30
(c) 36, 30 (d) None of these

46. 17, 23, 29, 35, ______, 47
(a) 40 (b) 41
(c) 42 (d) 43

47. A, G, L, P, S, ______
(a) U (b) X
(c) W (d) Y

48. L, O, G, T, B, ______
(a) N (b) Y
(c) Z (d) W

49. A, C, E, G, ______
(a) K (b) L
(c) H (d) I

50. D, G, J, M, ______
(a) P (b) O
(c) N (d) S

51. P, N, L, J, H, ______
(a) E (b) F
(c) G (d) I

52. I, F, C, Z, W, ______
(a) S (b) R
(c) T (d) Y

Direction (53–60) : Find the letter/word/number which is different from other alternatives.

53. (a) M (b) N
(c) A (d) P

54. (a) 20 (b) 21
(c) 22 (d) 23

55. (a) May (b) April
(c) Saturday (d) June

56. (a) Patna (b) Indore
(c) Bangladesh (d) Islamabad

57. (a) CD (b) MO
(c) KL (d) FG

58. (a) 37 (b) 48
(c) 46 (d) 52

59. (a) Earth (b) Mars
(c) Venus (d) Sun

60. (a) Minutes (b) Hours
(c) Days (d) Scale

Direction (61–67) : Find out the missing word or number.

61. Elbow : Hand : : Fingres : ?
(a) Palm (b) Foot
(c) Nails (d) Hand

62. 16 : 80 : : 18 : ?
(a) 85 (b) 86
(c) 90 (d) 95

63. Father : Mother : : Uncle : ?
(a) Sister (b) Aunt
(c) Mother-in-law (d) Daughter-in-law

64. India : New Delhi : : Bangladesh : ?
(a) Kathmandu (b) Islamabad
(c) Dhaka (d) Male

65. Guitar : Music : : Food : ?
(a) Energy (b) Run
(c) Jump (d) Rest

66. Dolphin : Sea : : Chicken : ?
(a) Burrow (b) Stable
(c) Hive (d) Coop

67. 1 week : 7 days : : 1 hour: ?
(a) 50 minutes (b) 56 minutes
(c) 60 minutes (d) 65 minutes

Direction (68–70) : Which of the following figures is hidden or embedded in the given figure?

68. 

(a) (b)

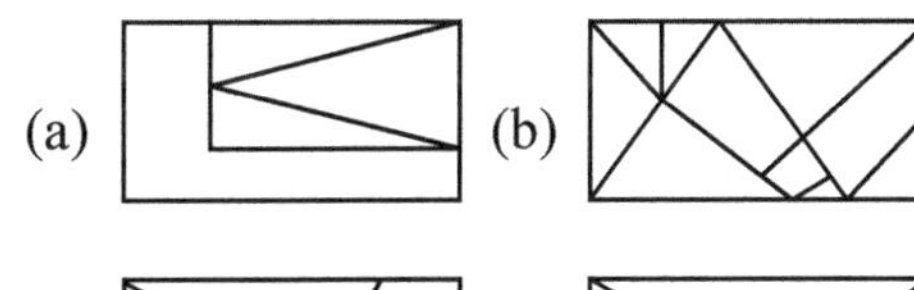

(c) (d)

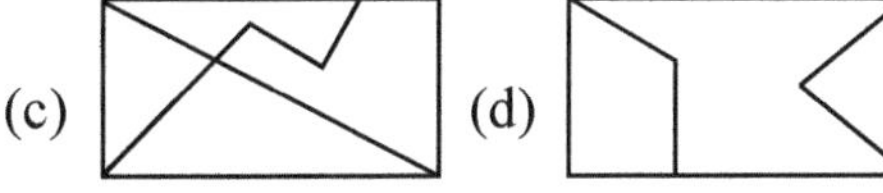

69. 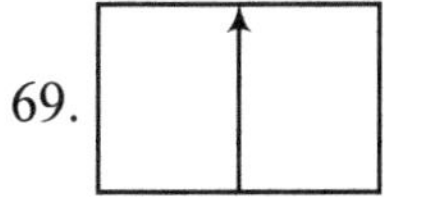

(a) (b)

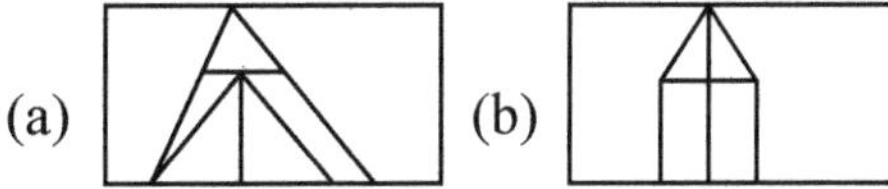

(c) 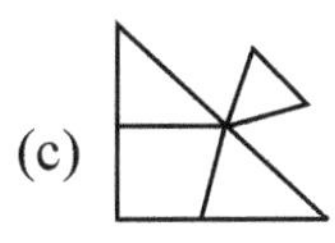 (d) None of these

70. 

(a) (b)

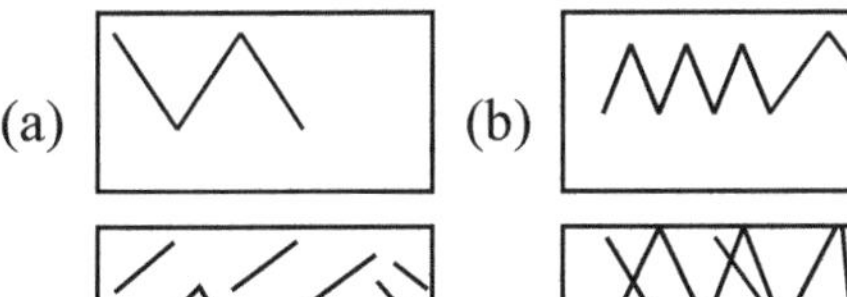

(c) (d)

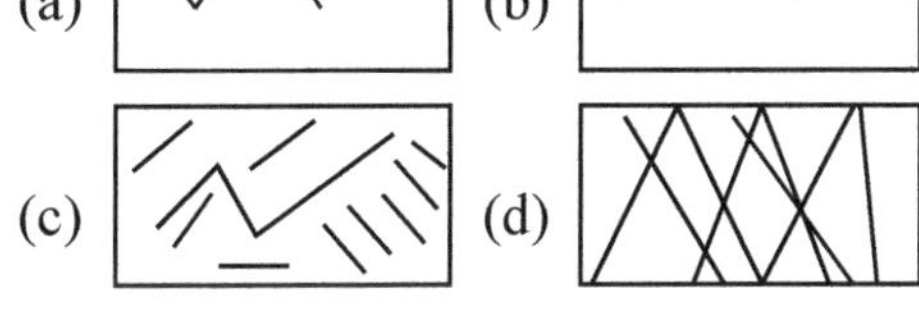

71. Complete the following series :

418, 422, 426, ______

(a) 436 (b) 435

(c) 430 (d) 432

72. How many triangles are there in the given figure?

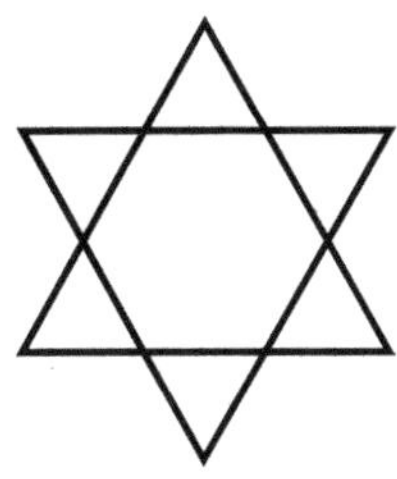

(a) 6 (b) 8

(c) 10 (d) 7

73. Which of the following figures do not touch at all?

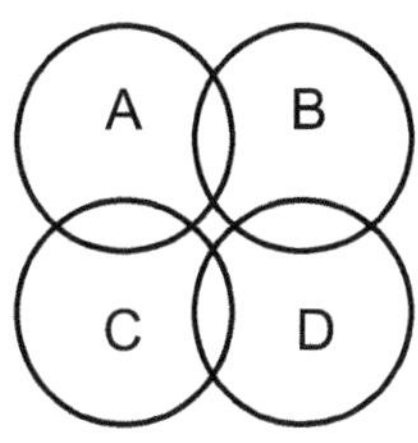

(a) (A) and (D)

(b) (C) and (B)

(c) Both (a) and (b)

(d) (B) and (D)

Direction (74–75) : Find the missing number in the following pattern :

74. 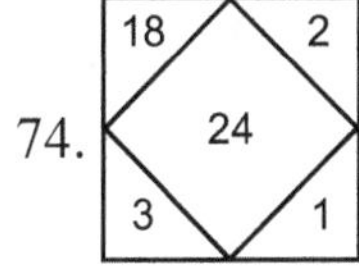

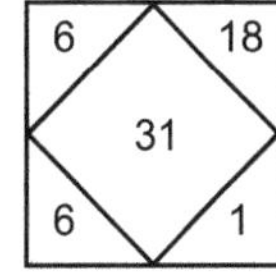

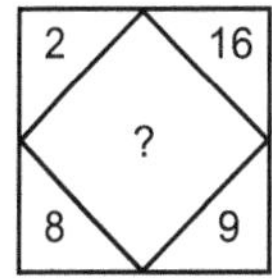

(a) 36 (b) 35

(c) 34 (d) 37

75. 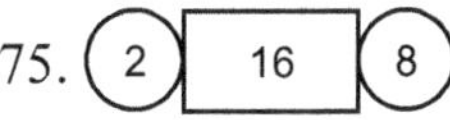

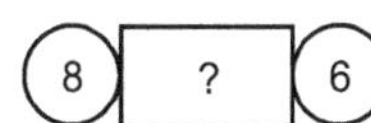

(a) 14 (b) 16

(c) 44 (d) 48

76. Which figure has the maximum number of corners?

(a) Triangle (b) Square

(c) Circle (d) Cube

77. Calendar : Date : : Dictionary : ?

(a) Word (b) Book

(c) Sentence (d) Copy

78. Find the letter which will end the first word and start the second word MA?, ?ENT

(a) K (b) T

(c) N (d) L

79. What will be the 11th shape in the pattern given below ?

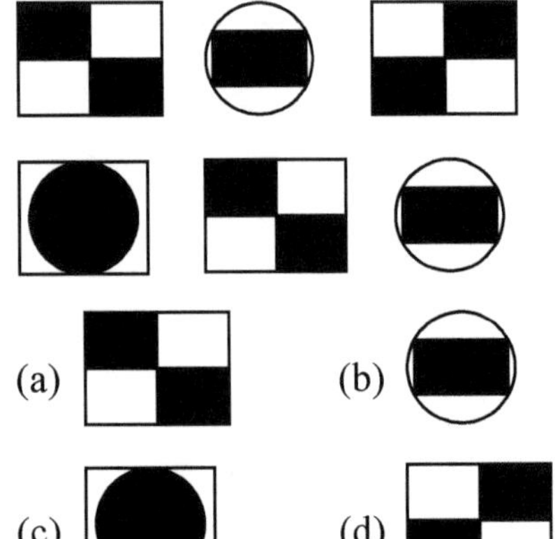

(a) (b) (c) (d)

80. Find the missing shape.

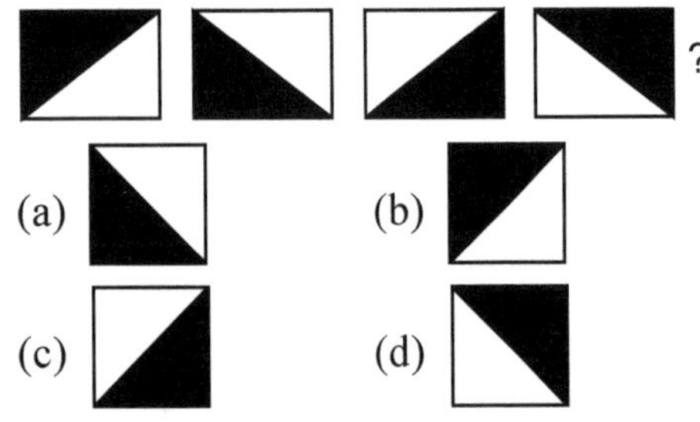

(a) (b) (c) (d)

81. Find the odd one out :

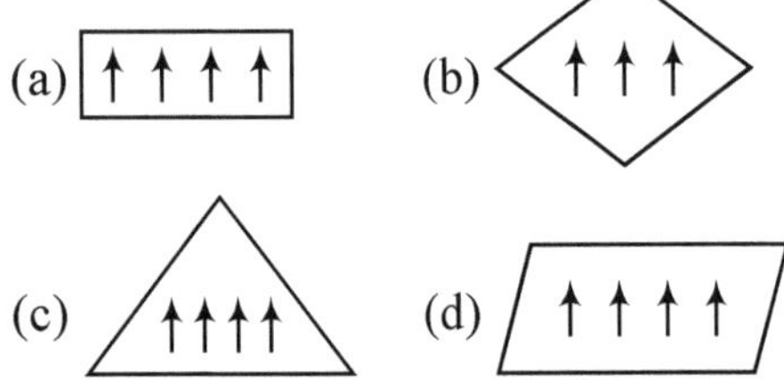

(a) (b) (c) (d)

82. Which of the following letters is fifth from right end in the given word?

MATHEMATICS

(a) A (b) E

(c) M (d) H

83. How many balls are outside the basket?

(a) 4 (b) 5

(c) 6 (d) 7

84. How many groups of 3 rats are there in the given figure?

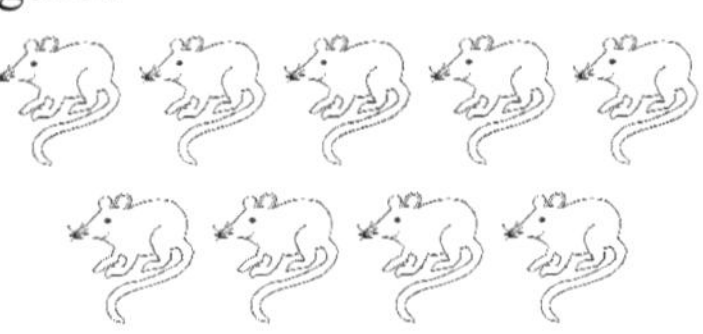

(a) 2 (b) 3

(c) 4 (d) 5

85. Which of the following is the thickest eraser?

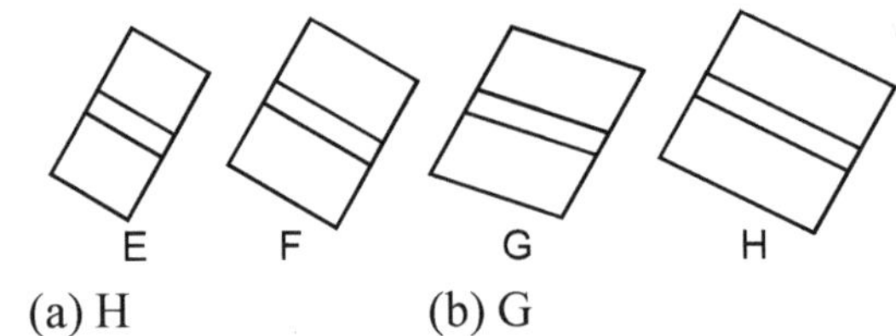

(a) H (b) G

(c) E (d) F

86. Complete the following number pattern.

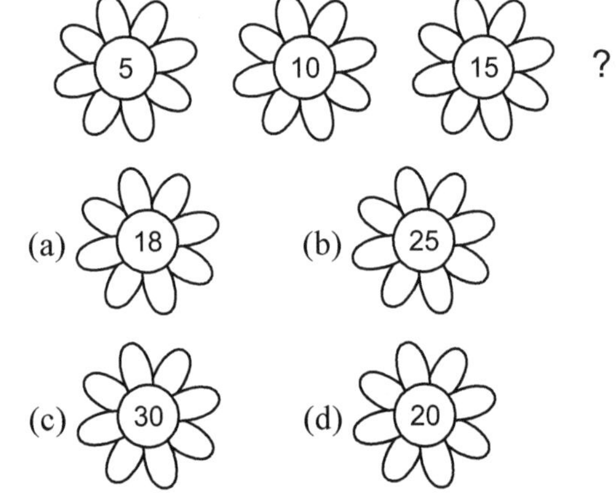

87. How many total number of squares are there in the given figure?

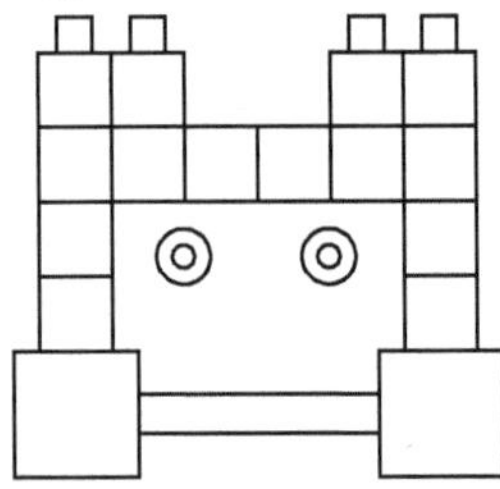

(a) 16 (b) 17

(c) 18 (d) None of these

88. Select the odd one out.

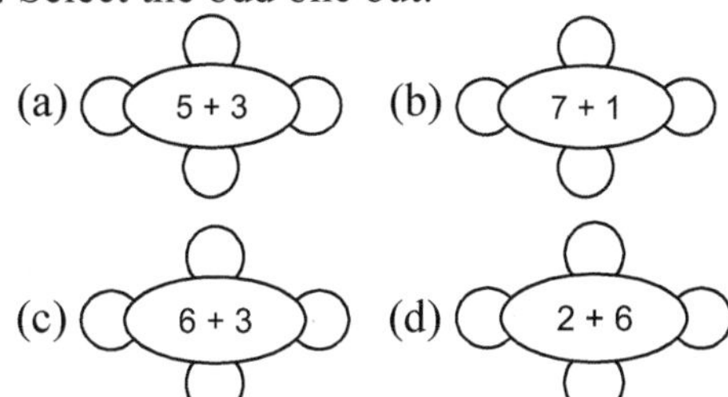

89. Complete the number pattern.

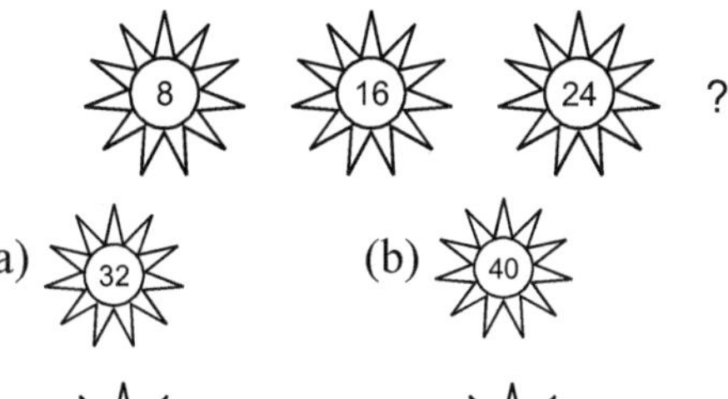

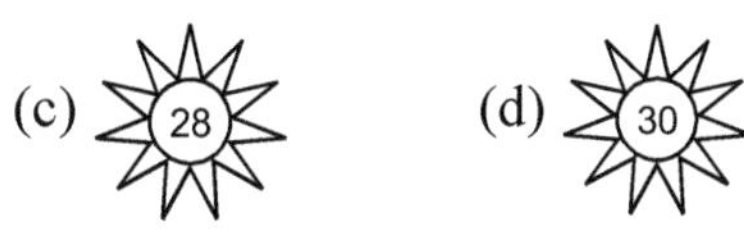

90. If 5 is related to [shape], then 4 is related to ______.

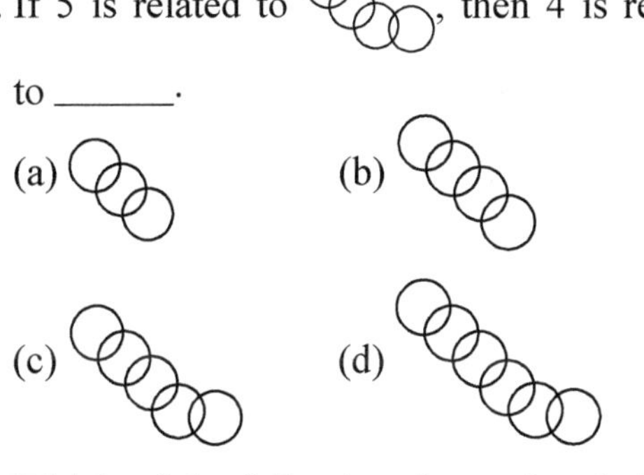

91. Which of the following shapes is missing in the given figure?

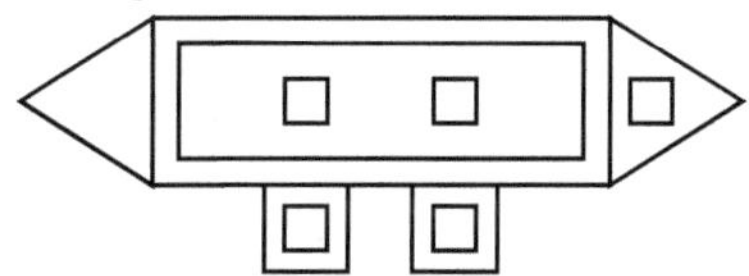

(a) Triangle (b) Circle
(c) Square (d) Rectangle

92. Which of the following is 4th ice-cream from left end?

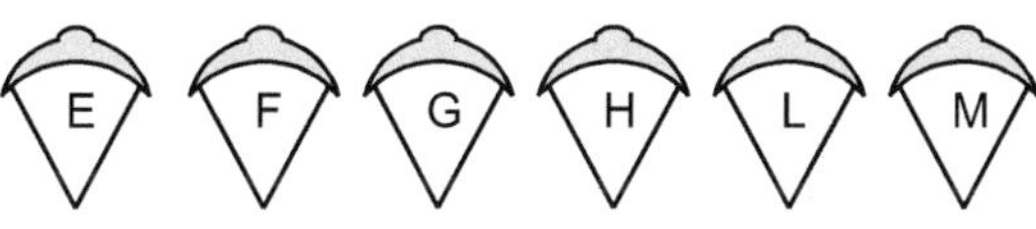

(a) H (b) G
(c) M (d) L

93. If yesterday was Monday, then tomorrow will be ______.

(a) Tuesday (b) Friday
(c) Wednesday (d) Thursday

94. To which group does the shape [shape] belong?

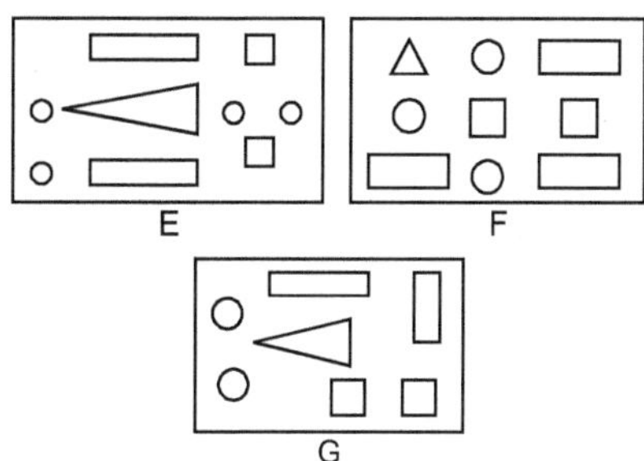

(a) E and G (b) E and F
(c) F and G (d) E, F and G

95. Find the odd one out.

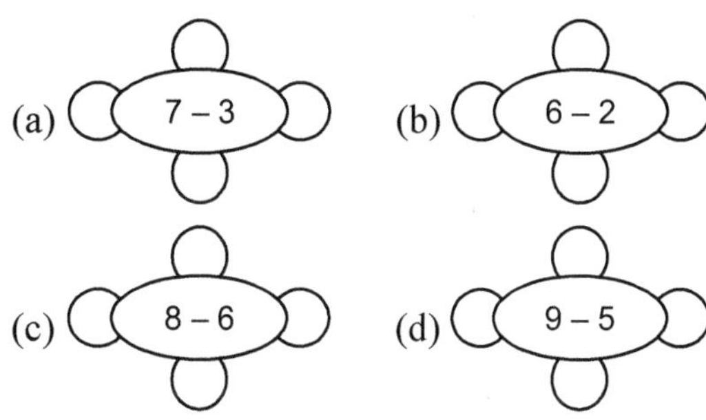

96. If 7 is related to [shape], then 3 is related to ______.

(a) (b)
(c) (d)

97. If [shape] is related to [shape], then [shape] is related to ______.

(a) 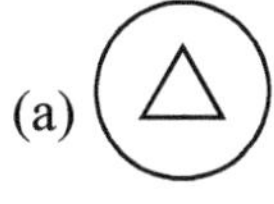
(b) 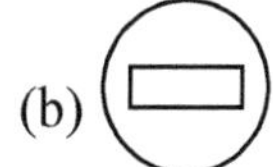
(c) 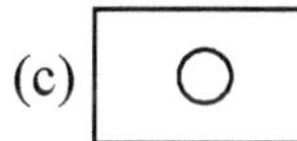
(d)

98. If tomorrow will be Thursday, then yesterday was ________.

(a) Monday (b) Sunday

(c) Tuesday (d) Wednesday

99. Which of the following is the tallest?

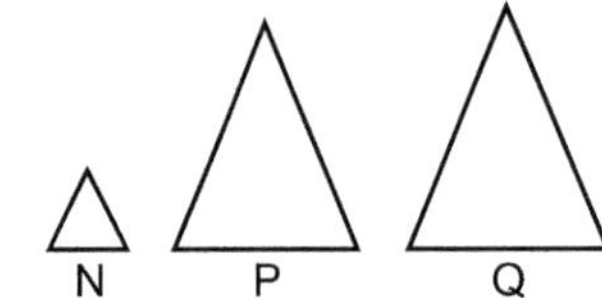

(a) P (b) Q

(c) L (d) M

100. How many balls are there in the box?

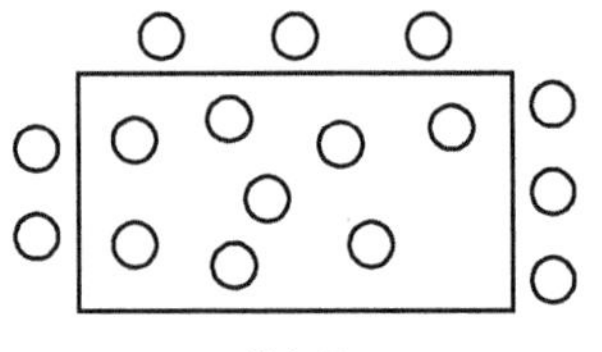
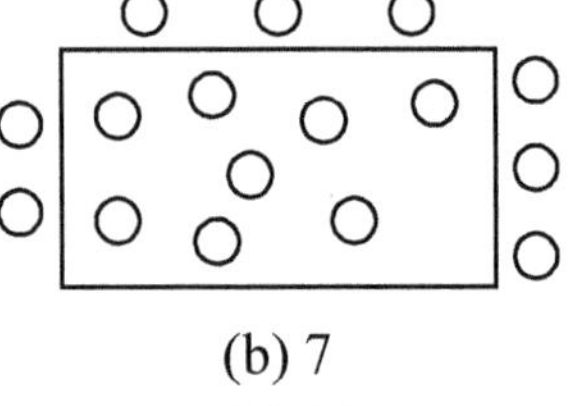

(a) 5 (b) 7

(c) 8 (d) 10

☺☺☺

Darken Your Choice with HB Pencil

1.	ⓐ	ⓑ	ⓒ	ⓓ	21.	ⓐ	ⓑ	ⓒ	ⓓ	41.	ⓐ	ⓑ	ⓒ	ⓓ	61.	ⓐ	ⓑ	ⓒ	ⓓ	81.	ⓐ	ⓑ	ⓒ	ⓓ
2.	ⓐ	ⓑ	ⓒ	ⓓ	22.	ⓐ	ⓑ	ⓒ	ⓓ	42.	ⓐ	ⓑ	ⓒ	ⓓ	62.	ⓐ	ⓑ	ⓒ	ⓓ	82.	ⓐ	ⓑ	ⓒ	ⓓ
3.	ⓐ	ⓑ	ⓒ	ⓓ	23.	ⓐ	ⓑ	ⓒ	ⓓ	43.	ⓐ	ⓑ	ⓒ	ⓓ	63.	ⓐ	ⓑ	ⓒ	ⓓ	83.	ⓐ	ⓑ	ⓒ	ⓓ
4.	ⓐ	ⓑ	ⓒ	ⓓ	24.	ⓐ	ⓑ	ⓒ	ⓓ	44.	ⓐ	ⓑ	ⓒ	ⓓ	64.	ⓐ	ⓑ	ⓒ	ⓓ	84.	ⓐ	ⓑ	ⓒ	ⓓ
5.	ⓐ	ⓑ	ⓒ	ⓓ	25.	ⓐ	ⓑ	ⓒ	ⓓ	45.	ⓐ	ⓑ	ⓒ	ⓓ	65.	ⓐ	ⓑ	ⓒ	ⓓ	85.	ⓐ	ⓑ	ⓒ	ⓓ
6.	ⓐ	ⓑ	ⓒ	ⓓ	26.	ⓐ	ⓑ	ⓒ	ⓓ	46.	ⓐ	ⓑ	ⓒ	ⓓ	66.	ⓐ	ⓑ	ⓒ	ⓓ	86.	ⓐ	ⓑ	ⓒ	ⓓ
7.	ⓐ	ⓑ	ⓒ	ⓓ	27.	ⓐ	ⓑ	ⓒ	ⓓ	47.	ⓐ	ⓑ	ⓒ	ⓓ	67.	ⓐ	ⓑ	ⓒ	ⓓ	87.	ⓐ	ⓑ	ⓒ	ⓓ
8.	ⓐ	ⓑ	ⓒ	ⓓ	28.	ⓐ	ⓑ	ⓒ	ⓓ	48.	ⓐ	ⓑ	ⓒ	ⓓ	68.	ⓐ	ⓑ	ⓒ	ⓓ	88.	ⓐ	ⓑ	ⓒ	ⓓ
9.	ⓐ	ⓑ	ⓒ	ⓓ	29.	ⓐ	ⓑ	ⓒ	ⓓ	49.	ⓐ	ⓑ	ⓒ	ⓓ	69.	ⓐ	ⓑ	ⓒ	ⓓ	89.	ⓐ	ⓑ	ⓒ	ⓓ
10.	ⓐ	ⓑ	ⓒ	ⓓ	30.	ⓐ	ⓑ	ⓒ	ⓓ	50.	ⓐ	ⓑ	ⓒ	ⓓ	70.	ⓐ	ⓑ	ⓒ	ⓓ	90.	ⓐ	ⓑ	ⓒ	ⓓ
11.	ⓐ	ⓑ	ⓒ	ⓓ	31.	ⓐ	ⓑ	ⓒ	ⓓ	51.	ⓐ	ⓑ	ⓒ	ⓓ	71.	ⓐ	ⓑ	ⓒ	ⓓ	91.	ⓐ	ⓑ	ⓒ	ⓓ
12.	ⓐ	ⓑ	ⓒ	ⓓ	32.	ⓐ	ⓑ	ⓒ	ⓓ	52.	ⓐ	ⓑ	ⓒ	ⓓ	72.	ⓐ	ⓑ	ⓒ	ⓓ	92.	ⓐ	ⓑ	ⓒ	ⓓ
13.	ⓐ	ⓑ	ⓒ	ⓓ	33.	ⓐ	ⓑ	ⓒ	ⓓ	53.	ⓐ	ⓑ	ⓒ	ⓓ	73.	ⓐ	ⓑ	ⓒ	ⓓ	93.	ⓐ	ⓑ	ⓒ	ⓓ
14.	ⓐ	ⓑ	ⓒ	ⓓ	34.	ⓐ	ⓑ	ⓒ	ⓓ	54.	ⓐ	ⓑ	ⓒ	ⓓ	74.	ⓐ	ⓑ	ⓒ	ⓓ	94.	ⓐ	ⓑ	ⓒ	ⓓ
15.	ⓐ	ⓑ	ⓒ	ⓓ	35.	ⓐ	ⓑ	ⓒ	ⓓ	55.	ⓐ	ⓑ	ⓒ	ⓓ	75.	ⓐ	ⓑ	ⓒ	ⓓ	95.	ⓐ	ⓑ	ⓒ	ⓓ
16.	ⓐ	ⓑ	ⓒ	ⓓ	36.	ⓐ	ⓑ	ⓒ	ⓓ	56.	ⓐ	ⓑ	ⓒ	ⓓ	76.	ⓐ	ⓑ	ⓒ	ⓓ	96.	ⓐ	ⓑ	ⓒ	ⓓ
17.	ⓐ	ⓑ	ⓒ	ⓓ	37.	ⓐ	ⓑ	ⓒ	ⓓ	57.	ⓐ	ⓑ	ⓒ	ⓓ	77.	ⓐ	ⓑ	ⓒ	ⓓ	97.	ⓐ	ⓑ	ⓒ	ⓓ
18.	ⓐ	ⓑ	ⓒ	ⓓ	38.	ⓐ	ⓑ	ⓒ	ⓓ	58.	ⓐ	ⓑ	ⓒ	ⓓ	78.	ⓐ	ⓑ	ⓒ	ⓓ	98.	ⓐ	ⓑ	ⓒ	ⓓ
19.	ⓐ	ⓑ	ⓒ	ⓓ	39.	ⓐ	ⓑ	ⓒ	ⓓ	59.	ⓐ	ⓑ	ⓒ	ⓓ	79.	ⓐ	ⓑ	ⓒ	ⓓ	99.	ⓐ	ⓑ	ⓒ	ⓓ
20.	ⓐ	ⓑ	ⓒ	ⓓ	40.	ⓐ	ⓑ	ⓒ	ⓓ	60.	ⓐ	ⓑ	ⓒ	ⓓ	80.	ⓐ	ⓑ	ⓒ	ⓓ	100.	ⓐ	ⓑ	ⓒ	ⓓ

WORKBOOK

Achievers Section

Multiple Choice Questions

1. How many two-digit numbers are there?
   (a) 99 (b) 89
   (c) 90 (d) 80
2. How many two-digit odd numbers are there?
   (a) 46 (b) 44
   (c) 45 (d) 48
3. What is the difference between the largest 2 digit number and the smallest one digit number?
   (a) 90 (b) 98
   (c) 9 (d) 1
4. What is the ordinal number of 7?
   (a) Fifth (b) Sixth
   (c) Eighth (d) Seventh
5. How many numbers lie between 27 and 37?
   (a) 9 (b) 10
   (c) 18 (d) 12
6. How many stars are there in the given figure?

   (a) 7 (b) 8
   (c) 9 (d) 6
7. 1 tens + 5 tens + 2 ones = ______.
   (a) 52 (b) 72
   (c) 62 (d) 42
8. Shyam has 21 chocolates. Ravi has 4 chocolates more than Shyam. How many chocolates they have in total?
   (a) 25 (b) 46
   (c) 42 (d) 44
9. A boy jumps 2 steps towards right from 3, and then 1 step towards right from there. Where will he reach?

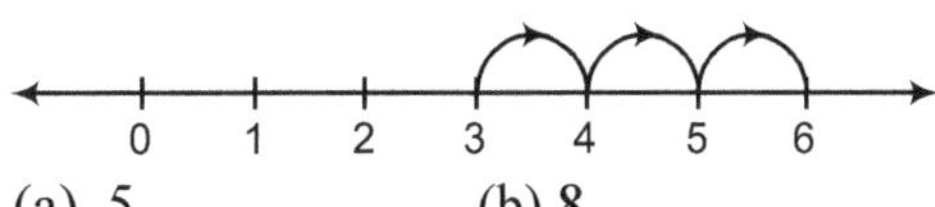

   (a) 5 (b) 8
   (c) 6 (d) 7
10. Which of the following shows the least value?

(a)	11 tens + 2 ones	(b)	12 tens – 2 ones
(c)	11 tens – 8 ones	(d)	10 tens + 6 ones

11. 10 persons share 40 mangoes equally. How many mangoes did each of them get?
   (a) 20 (b) 25
   (c) 18 (d) 16
12. If each O weighs 1 kg, then the weight of Ram is ________.

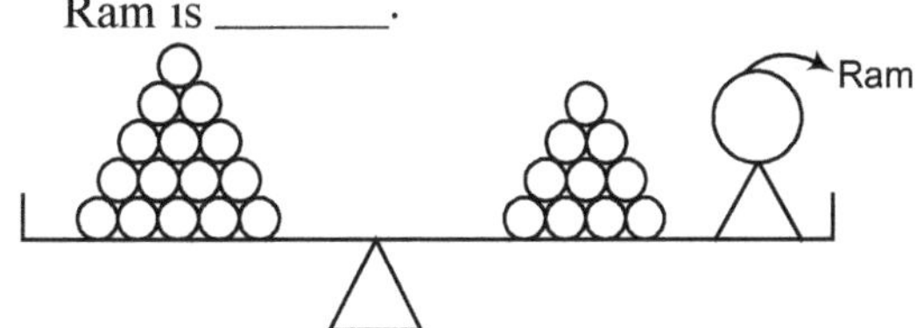

   (a) 10 kg (b) 5 kg
   (c) 7 kg (d) 8 kg

13. How many faces does a sphere have?
(a) 2 (b) 1
(c) 3 (d) 4

14. How many circles are outside the triangle in the given figure?

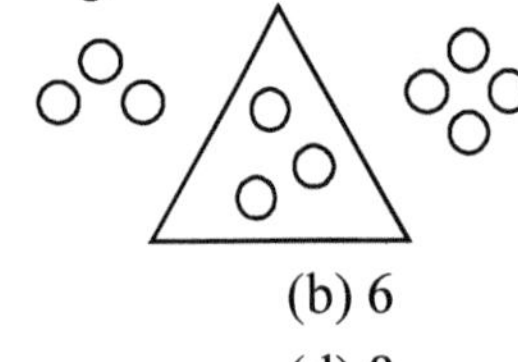

(a) 3 (b) 6
(c) 7 (d) 8

15. Which of the following months lie between November and March?
(a) April (b) June
(c) May (d) February

16. Which of the following clocks shows 8'o clock?

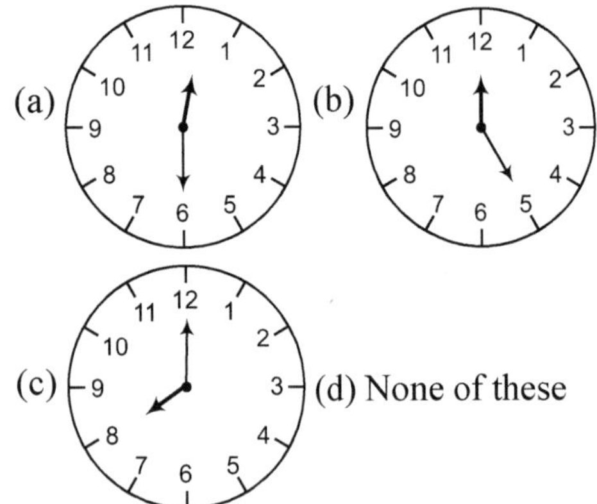

(a) (b)
(c) (d) None of these

17. How many months of any year have 30 days?
(a) 4 (b) 6
(c) 8 (d) 9

18. If □ = 25, and ○ = 11, then what is the value of □ – ○?
(a) 16 (b) 17
(c) 14 (d) 15

19. A book has 26 pages. Parineeti read 11 pages. How many pages are left to be read?
(a) 11 (b) 13
(c) 17 (d) 15

20. How many weeks are there in a year?
(a) 58 (b) 57
(c) 56 (d) 52

21. How many complete days are there in 50 hours?
(a) 2 (b) 3
(c) 4 (d) 5

22. The hour hand of a clock repeats its position, after every ________.
(a) 1 hour (b) 5 hours
(c) 6 hours (d) 12 hours

23. If a month of 30 days starts with Sunday, what will be the last day of the month?
(a) Tuesday (b) Monday
(c) Wednesday (d) Friday

24. How many days are there in 3 weeks?
(a) 28 (b) 21
(c) 26 (d) 24

25. If the last day of February of a leap year is Monday, then what will be the first day of February, of the same year?
(a) Monday (b) Tuesday
(c) Wednesday (d) Sunday.

26. Ram has ₹ 24. He lost ₹ 10, then how much money is left with Ram?
(a) ₹ 10 (b) ₹ 14
(c) ₹ 34 (d) ₹ 32

27. Rahim has four 50 rupees and two 10 rupees notes. How much money does Rahim have?
(a) ₹ 210 (b) ₹ 220
(c) ₹ 120 (d) ₹ 110

28. From what 23 is subtracted to get 17?
(a) 37 (b) 6
(c) 40 (d) 16

29. Water is to be filled in the container Q. How many containers of P can fill Q completely?

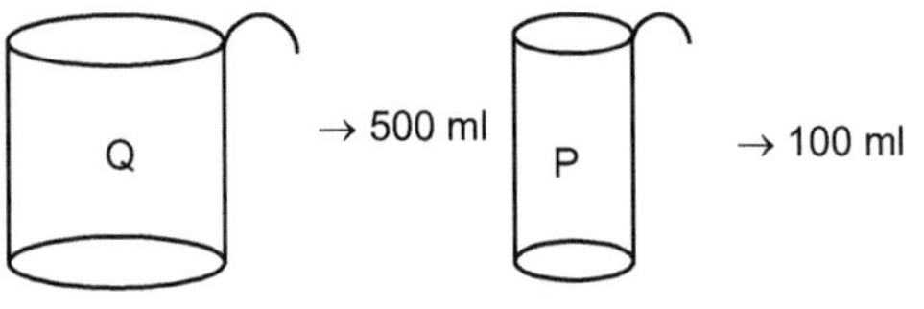

(a) 6 (b) 5
(c) 8 (d) 10

30. Which of the following is the lightest?
(a) Pencil (b) Book
(c) Paperweight (d) School bag

31. 2 tens 3 ones – 4 ones = ...tens ......ones.
(a) 2, 1 (b) 1, 8
(c) 1, 9 (d) 1, 7

32. A shopkeeper sold 25 bags on Monday. He sold 5 bags less on Tuesday. How many bags are sold on Tuesday?
(a) 20 (b) 26
(c) 15 (d) 21

33. What should be added to 13 to get 27?
(a) 13 (b) 14
(c) 15 (d) 16

34. Rohan's class started at 5 : 30 pm and its duration was 30 minutes, when will his class end?
(a) 6 : 00 pm (b) 6 : 00 am
(c) 5 : 00 pm (d) 5 : 20 am

35. How many millilitres are there in a half litre?
(a) 300 (b) 700
(c) 500 (d) 1000

36. How many millimetres make one metre?
(a) 10 (b) 100
(c) 1000 (d) 10000

37. The weight of a box of sweets is 2 kg. How many such sweet boxes weigh 18 kg?
(a) 8 (b) 9
(c) 7 (d) 6

38. Building P Q R

Which of the following is the nearest to the building?
(a) P (b) Q
(c) R (d) Both (a) and (b)

39. Jai is waiting for the school bus. He is standing third from the right end and 8th from the left end in the queue. How many boys are there in the queue?
(a) 9 (b) 10
(c) 12 (d) 20

40. Mohan has two 100-rupees notes. He bought a toy car of ₹ 40. What is the amount of money left with Mohan?
(a) ₹ 60 (b) ₹ 80
(c) ₹ 170 (d) ₹ 160

☺☺☺

Darken Your Choice with HB Pencil

1.	ⓐ	ⓑ	ⓒ	ⓓ	9.	ⓐ	ⓑ	ⓒ	ⓓ	17.	ⓐ	ⓑ	ⓒ	ⓓ	25.	ⓐ	ⓑ	ⓒ	ⓓ	33.	ⓐ	ⓑ	ⓒ	ⓓ
2.	ⓐ	ⓑ	ⓒ	ⓓ	10.	ⓐ	ⓑ	ⓒ	ⓓ	18.	ⓐ	ⓑ	ⓒ	ⓓ	26.	ⓐ	ⓑ	ⓒ	ⓓ	34.	ⓐ	ⓑ	ⓒ	ⓓ
3.	ⓐ	ⓑ	ⓒ	ⓓ	11.	ⓐ	ⓑ	ⓒ	ⓓ	19.	ⓐ	ⓑ	ⓒ	ⓓ	27.	ⓐ	ⓑ	ⓒ	ⓓ	35.	ⓐ	ⓑ	ⓒ	ⓓ
4.	ⓐ	ⓑ	ⓒ	ⓓ	12.	ⓐ	ⓑ	ⓒ	ⓓ	20.	ⓐ	ⓑ	ⓒ	ⓓ	28.	ⓐ	ⓑ	ⓒ	ⓓ	36.	ⓐ	ⓑ	ⓒ	ⓓ
5.	ⓐ	ⓑ	ⓒ	ⓓ	13.	ⓐ	ⓑ	ⓒ	ⓓ	21.	ⓐ	ⓑ	ⓒ	ⓓ	29.	ⓐ	ⓑ	ⓒ	ⓓ	37.	ⓐ	ⓑ	ⓒ	ⓓ
6.	ⓐ	ⓑ	ⓒ	ⓓ	14.	ⓐ	ⓑ	ⓒ	ⓓ	22.	ⓐ	ⓑ	ⓒ	ⓓ	30.	ⓐ	ⓑ	ⓒ	ⓓ	38.	ⓐ	ⓑ	ⓒ	ⓓ
7.	ⓐ	ⓑ	ⓒ	ⓓ	15.	ⓐ	ⓑ	ⓒ	ⓓ	23.	ⓐ	ⓑ	ⓒ	ⓓ	31.	ⓐ	ⓑ	ⓒ	ⓓ	39.	ⓐ	ⓑ	ⓒ	ⓓ
8.	ⓐ	ⓑ	ⓒ	ⓓ	16.	ⓐ	ⓑ	ⓒ	ⓓ	24.	ⓐ	ⓑ	ⓒ	ⓓ	32.	ⓐ	ⓑ	ⓒ	ⓓ	40.	ⓐ	ⓑ	ⓒ	ⓓ

WORKBOOK

Hints and Solutions

1. NUMBER SENSE

Answer Key

1. (b)	2. (b)	3. (b)	4. (d)	5. (a)	6. (b)	7. (c)	8. (d)	9. (a)	10. (b)
11. (a)	12. (c)	13. (b)	14. (a)	15. (a)	16. (b)	17. (a)	18. (b)	19. (b)	20. (d)
21. (a)	22. (b)	23. (a)	24. (a)	25. (a)	26. (d)	27. (c)	28. (a)	29. (b)	30. (c)
31. (d)	32. (d)	33. (b)	34. (c)	35. (b)	36. (a)	37. (b)	38. (c)	39. (a)	40. (d)
41. (b)	42. (b)	43. (c)	44. (d)	45. (d)	46. (b)	47. (d)	48. (c)	49. (b)	50. (c)
51. (b)	52. (a)	53. (c)	54. (c)	55. (b)	56. (a)	57. (c)	58. (b)	59. (c)	60. (a)

41. 78 comes between 77 and 79.

42. Counting by 3's means adding 3 to previous number

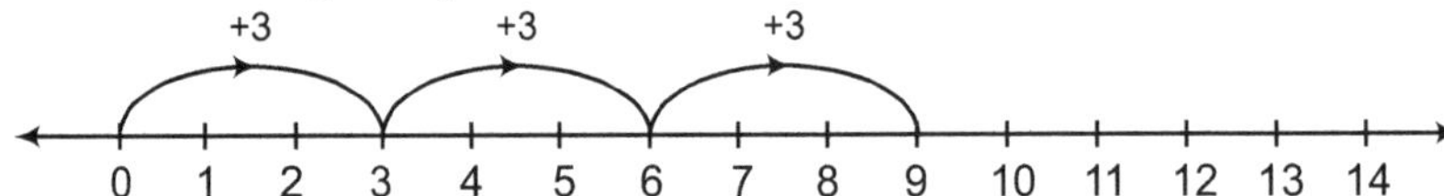

44. Priya = 53, Banti = 65, Nancy = 39, Sonu = 81

    81 is the largest among the given numbers.

45. The order in ascending pattern is:

    $17 < 29 < 39 < 52 < 76$

46. Jar b has 6 balls which is least.

47. There are 12 rats in the given picture.

48. Maximum number of apples = 8

49. The number lying between 60 and 70 and having 8 at ones place = 68

51. Counting by 2's means adding 2 to previous number.

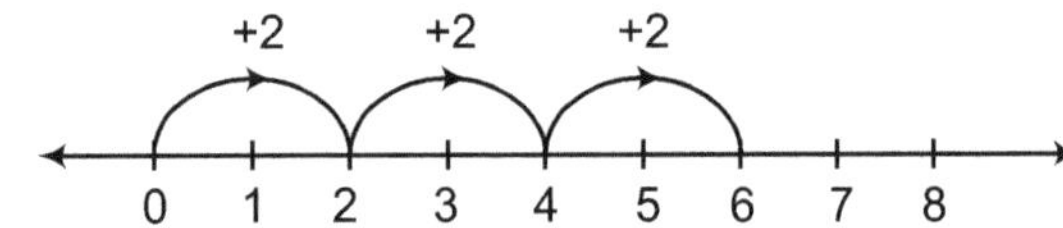

52. 4 tens 9 ones = 40 + 9 = 49

53. 89 comes between 88 and 90.

54. The numbers in descending order

    $61 > 57 > 48 > 45$

55. 59 comes between 58 and 60.

57. Manoj = 34, Manju = 71, Raju = 62, Rani = 46

    34 is the smallest number among them.

58. 43 + 1 = 44

59. Counting by 2's means adding 2 to previous number.

60. 66 comes between 65 and 67.

2. ADDITION

Answer Key

1. (d)	2. (b)	3. (a)	4. (c)	5. (d)	6. (a)	7. (a)	8. (b)	9. (c)	10. (d)
11. (a)	12. (d)	13. (c)	14. (d)	15. (b)	16. (a)	17. (b)	18. (c)	19. (b)	20. (c)
21. (d)	22. (c)	23. (b)	24. (c)	25. (d)	26. (a)	27. (a)	28. (d)	29. (b)	30. (c)
31. (a)	32. (d)	33. (b)	34. (d)	35. (a)	36. (d)	37. (c)	38. (c)	39. (b)	40. (a)
41. (a)	42. (c)	43. (c)	44. (b)	45. (b)	46. (a)	47. (c)	48. (c)	49. (b)	50. (b)
51. (a)	52. (b)	53. (c)	54. (b)	55. (b)	56. (a)	57. (c)	58. (d)	59. (b)	60. (c)

41. $\begin{array}{r} 5\ 0 \\ +\boxed{0} \\ \hline 5\ 0 \end{array}$

42. $\begin{array}{r} 1\ 8 \\ +\boxed{09} \\ \hline 2\ 7 \end{array}$

43. $\begin{array}{r} 1\ 3 \\ +1\ 9 \\ \hline 3\ 2 \end{array}$ $\quad \begin{array}{r} 2\ 7 \\ +1\ 5 \\ \hline 4\ 2 \end{array}$ $\quad \begin{array}{r} 3\ 6 \\ +1\ 3 \\ \hline 4\ 9 \end{array}$ $\quad \begin{array}{r} 1\ 8 \\ +2\ 1 \\ \hline 3\ 9 \end{array}$

44. $\begin{array}{r} 3\ 1 \\ +2\ 6 \\ \hline 5\ 7 \end{array}$ $\quad \begin{array}{r} 3\ 2 \\ +2\ 7 \\ \hline 5\ 9 \end{array}$ $\quad \begin{array}{r} 2\ 6 \\ +2\ 5 \\ \hline 5\ 1 \end{array}$ $\quad \begin{array}{r} 1\ 8 \\ +3\ 1 \\ \hline 4\ 9 \end{array}$

45. Number of parrots = 9
 Number of pigeons = 8
 Number of hens = 8
 Number of chicks = 5
 Total number of birds = 9 + 8 + 8 + 5 = 30

46. Number of toys bought on Sunday = 17
 Number of toys bought on Monday = 9
 Number of toys bought on Tuesday = 12
 Total number of toys bought = 17 + 9 + 12
 = 38

47. Total number of chocolates = 46 + 7 = 53

48. $\begin{array}{r} 3\ 7 \\ +4\ 2 \\ \hline 7\ 9 \end{array}$ $\quad \begin{array}{r} 4\ 6 \\ +2\ 3 \\ \hline 6\ 9 \end{array}$ $\quad \begin{array}{r} 5\ 8 \\ +3\ 1 \\ \hline 8\ 9 \end{array}$ $\quad \begin{array}{r} 3\ 5 \\ +4\ 2 \\ \hline 7\ 7 \end{array}$

49. $\begin{array}{r} 5\ 2 \\ +\ \ 7 \\ \hline 5\ 9 \end{array}$ $\quad \begin{array}{r} 5\ 1 \\ +\ \ 3 \\ \hline 5\ 4 \end{array}$ $\quad \begin{array}{r} 5\ 1 \\ +\ \ 8 \\ \hline 5\ 9 \end{array}$ $\quad \begin{array}{r} 6\ 2 \\ +\ \ 7 \\ \hline 6\ 9 \end{array}$

50. $\begin{array}{r} 7\ 2 \\ +\ \ 4 \\ \hline 7\ 6 \end{array}$ $\quad \begin{array}{r} 8\ 3 \\ +\ \ 5 \\ \hline 8\ 8 \end{array}$ $\quad \begin{array}{r} 6\ 4 \\ +\ \ 3 \\ \hline 6\ 7 \end{array}$ $\quad \begin{array}{r} 8\ 2 \\ +\ \ 3 \\ \hline 8\ 5 \end{array}$

51. $\begin{array}{r} 1\ 6 \\ +\ \ 5 \\ \hline 2\ 1 \end{array}$ $\quad \begin{array}{r} 2\ 3 \\ +\ \ 4 \\ \hline 2\ 7 \end{array}$ $\quad \begin{array}{r} 3\ 6 \\ +\ \ 3 \\ \hline 3\ 9 \end{array}$ $\quad \begin{array}{r} 4\ 1 \\ +\ \ 6 \\ \hline 4\ 7 \end{array}$

 Largest to smallest 47 > 39 > 27 > 21
 H > G > F > E

52. 5 + 8 = 13, 6 + 9 = 15, 5 + 9 = 14, 6 + 8 = 14

53. 12 + 4 = 16 = 1 Ten + 6 Ones

54. 20 ones + 5 tens = 20 + 50 = 70
 6 tens + 7 ones = 60 + 7 = 67
 4 tens + 3 tens = 40 + 30 = 70
 7 tens + 6 ones = 70 + 6 = 76

55. $\begin{array}{r} 5\ 3 \\ +2\ 3 \\ \hline 7\ 6 \end{array}$

 50 + 3 = 53
 20 + 3 = 23

56. Total number of flowers in set M and N

= 14 + 15 = 29

57. Total number of flowers in set L and N

= 12 + 15 = 27

58. Total number of flowers in all the sets

= 12 + 14 + 15 = 41

59.
$$\begin{array}{r} 17 \\ +31 \\ \hline 48 \\ \hline \end{array} \quad \begin{array}{r} 25 \\ +13 \\ \hline 38 \\ \hline \end{array} \quad \begin{array}{r} 28 \\ +11 \\ \hline 39 \\ \hline \end{array} \quad \begin{array}{r} 32 \\ +13 \\ \hline 45 \\ \hline \end{array}$$

60. Total number of animals = 15 + 11 + 22 = 48

3. SUBTRACTION

Answer Key

1. (d)	2. (d)	3. (b)	4. (c)	5. (d)	6. (b)	7. (d)	8. (b)	9. (d)	10. (b)
11. (c)	12. (b)	13. (d)	14. (a)	15. (c)	16. (d)	17. (b)	18. (b)	19. (a)	20. (d)
21. (b)	22. (a)	23. (c)	24. (c)	25. (b)	26. (c)	27. (d)	28. (c)	29. (d)	30. (a)
31. (a)	32. (b)	33. (a)	34. (b)	35. (a)	36. (a)	37. (b)	38. (a)	39. (c)	40. (d)
41. (b)	42. (d)	43. (c)	44. (c)	45. (a)	46. (b)	47. (a)	48. (a)	49. (a)	50. (a)
51. (b)	52. (b)	53. (b)	54. (a)	55. (a)	56. (b)	57. (a)	58. (c)	59. (d)	60. (a)

41.
$$\begin{array}{r} 67 \\ -20 \\ \hline 47 \\ \hline \end{array} \quad \begin{array}{r} 52 \\ -30 \\ \hline 22 \\ \hline \end{array} \quad \begin{array}{r} 43 \\ -\ \ 2 \\ \hline 41 \\ \hline \end{array} \quad \begin{array}{r} 53 \\ -12 \\ \hline 41 \\ \hline \end{array}$$

42. 8 – 5 = 3

12 – 7 = 5; 13 – 8 = 5; 11 – 4 = 7; 12 – 9 = 3

43. 17 – 17 = 0, 38 – 16 = 22, 73 – 31 = 42,

87 – 25 = 62

44.
$$\begin{array}{r} 37 \\ -15 \\ \hline 22 \\ \hline \end{array}$$

45.
$$\begin{array}{r} 18 \\ -\ \ 7 \\ \hline 11 \\ \hline \end{array}$$

46. 23 + 42 = 65

$$\begin{array}{r} 90 \\ -65 \\ \hline 25 \\ \hline \end{array}$$

47. 19 – 7 = 12

48.
$$\begin{array}{r} 45 \\ -23 \\ \hline 22 \\ \hline \end{array}$$

49. 26 – 5 = 21

50. 45 – 33 = 12

51. M = 6 + 2 = 8

N = 4 + 3 = 7

52.
$$\begin{array}{r} 47 \\ -15 \\ \hline 32 \\ \hline \end{array} = 3 \text{ tens and } 2 \text{ ones}$$

53. 18 – 2 = 6

19 – 12 = 7, 38 – 32 = 6, 39 – 36 = 3

27 – 22 = 5

56.
$$\begin{array}{r} 97 \\ -53 \\ \hline 44 \\ \hline \end{array}$$

57. 5 tens 9 ones = 59

3 tens 7 ones = 37

$$\begin{array}{r} 59 \\ -37 \\ \hline 22 \\ \hline \end{array}$$

58. Greatest number = 96

Smallest number = 13

$$\begin{array}{r} 96 \\ 13 \\ \hline 83 \\ \hline \end{array}$$

59. Largest number = 98

Smallest number = 14

$$\begin{array}{r} 98 \\ -14 \\ \hline 84 \\ \hline \end{array}$$

60. Largest number = 96

Second largest number = 92

$$\begin{array}{r} 96 \\ -92 \\ \hline 04 \\ \hline \end{array}$$

4. MEASUREMENT

Answer Key

1. (a)	2. (d)	3. (b)	4. (b)	5. (a)	6. (b)	7. (b)	8. (d)	9. (c)	10. (b)
11. (a)	12. (b)	13. (c)	14. (a)	15. (a)	16. (a)	17. (a)	18. (b)	19. (a)	20. (d)
21. (a)	22. (c)	23. (b)	24. (d)	25. (c)	26. (a)	27. (d)	28. (c)	29. (a)	30. (b)
31. (c)	32. (a)	33. (b)	34. (d)	35. (a)	36. (a)	37. (a)	38. (a)	39. (c)	40. (a)
41. (b)	42. (d)	43. (d)	44. (c)	45. (a)	46. (b)	47. (c)	48. (a)	49. (b)	50. (d)

41. Rohit's weight = 28 – 5 = 23 kg

42. Weight of flour bag = 4 kg

$4 + 4 + 4 + 4 + 4 = 20$ kg

43. 10 + 10 = 20 marbles

44. Total length of combs = 4 + 5 = 9 units

45. Mango is heaviest.

46. Length of gun = (2 + 2 + 2 + 2 + 2 + 2) = 12

48. Length of pencil = 12 – 3 = 9 cm.

Length of P = 9 cm

49. Monu is taller than Mini and shorter than Nilu.

50. Balloon S has longest string.

5. TIME

Answer Key

1. (a)	2. (c)	3. (b)	4. (a)	5. (b)	6. (b)	7. (d)	8. (b)	9. (c)	10. (b)
11. (a)	12. (c)	13. (a)	14. (c)	15. (b)	16. (b)	17. (b)	18. (a)	19. (d)	20. (b)
21. (c)	22. (d)	23. (c)	24. (c)	25. (b)	26. (a)	27. (a)	28. (b)	29. (c)	30. (d)
31. (c)	32. (a)	33. (b)	34. (b)	35. (d)	36. (a)	37. (b)	38. (c)	39. (a)	40. (c)
41. (c)	42. (b)	43. (a)	44. (c)	45. (d)	46. (b)	47. (b)	48. (d)	49. (c)	50. (b)
51. (a)	52. (c)	53. (d)	54. (b)	55. (b)	56. (a)	57. (b)	58. (a)	59. (a)	

41. Sunday is always a holiday.
42. 7th month of a year is July.
43. In 2017, February has 28 days.
44. The months having 31 days are January, March, May, July, August, October, December.
45. Second month is February and tenth month is October. The months between them are March, April, May, June, July, August, September. There are 7 months.
46. 11th month is November.
    Month before November is October.
48. 28 = 7 + 7 + 7 +7
    There are four weeks.
49. Months after June and before October are July, August and September.
50. There are 52 weeks in a leap year.
51. Months after March and before August are April, May, June, July
52. In 7 weeks = 7 + 7 +7 +7 +7 +7 + 7 = 49 days
53. Today = Monday, yesterday = Sunday
    Day before yesterday = Saturday
54. 6th month of year is June.
56. Day before yesterday = Thursday
    Today = Saturday
    Tomorrow = Sunday
    Day after tomorrow = Monday
57. In 3 months = 31 + 31 + 31 = 93 days
58. September, October, November.

6. MONEY

Answer Key

1. (a)	2. (a)	3. (c)	4. (c)	5. (a)	6. (b)	7. (d)	8. (c)	9. (b)	10. (d)
11. (a)	12. (b)	13. (c)	14. (d)	15. (b)	16. (d)	17. (d)	18. (a)	19. (a)	20. (c)
21. (a)	22. (b)	23. (c)	24. (d)	25. (a)	26. (d)	27. (a)	28. (d)	29. (a)	30. (b)
31. (a)	32. (c)	33. (c)	34. (c)	35. (a)	36. (c)	37. (b)	38. (b)	39. (a)	40. (b)
41. (d)	42. (c)	43. (c)	44. (a)						

5. 60 – 30 = 30
6. 120 ÷ 40 = 3
7. 5 × 5 = 25
8. 1000 ÷ 200 = 5
9. 1500 ÷ 150 = 10
10. 100 – 40 = 60
11. 500 – 50 = 450
12. 10 × 5 = 50
14. 250 ÷ 50 = 5
22. 32 × 5 = 160
25. 70 ÷ 35 = 2
28. 3000 ÷ 500 = 6
29. 400 ÷ 40 = 10
30. 2.50 – 2.00 = 0.50 = 50 Paise
31. 2 + 2 + 5 + 1 = 10
32. 30 + 30 = ₹ 60
34. Money left with Aman = 50 – (10 + 20)
    = 50 – 30 = ₹ 20
36. 5 + 5 + 5 + 5 + 5 + 5 + 5 + 5 + 5 + 5 + 5 + 5 + 5 + 5 + 5 + 5 = 80
    There are 16 ₹ 5 notes.
37. 50 – 38 = ₹ 12
38. 20 + 20 + 20 = ₹ 60
39. Price of 2 pencils = 2 + 2 = 4
    Price of 1 balloon = 3
    Total = 4 + 3 = ₹ 7
40. Cost of 3 toffees = 2 + 2 + 2 = ₹ 6
    Cost of 2 ice-creams = 5 + 5 = ₹ 10
    Total = 6 + 10 = ₹ 16
41. Cost of 2 pens = 7 + 7 = 14
    Cost of 3 balloons = 3 + 3 + 3 = 9
    Total = 14 + 9 = ₹ 23
42. Cost of 3 ice-creams = 5 + 5 + 5 = ₹ 15
    Cost of 4 pencils = 2 + 2 + 2 + 2 = ₹ 8
    Total 15 + 8 = ₹ 23
43. Cost of 5 balloons = 3 + 3 + 3 + 3 + 3 = 15
    Cost of 6 Pencils = 2 + 2 + 2 + 2 + 2 + 2 = 12
    Total = 15 + 12 = ₹ 27
44. Cost of 5 toffees = 2 + 2 + 2 + 2 + 2 = ₹ 10
    Cost of 2 pens = 7 + 7 = ₹ 14
    Total = 10 + 14 = ₹ 24

7. GEOMETRICAL SHAPES

Answer Key

1. (c)	2. (b)	3. (a)	4. (c)	5. (b)	6. (c)	7. (b)	8. (a)	9. (c)	10. (b)
11. (d)	12. (c)	13. (a)	14. (b)	15. (d)	16. (c)	17. (a)	18. (d)	19. (d)	20. (a)
21. (b)	22. (c)	23. (d)	24. (d)	25. (b)	26. (d)	27. (a)	28. (a)	29. (d)	30. (c)
31. (b)	32. (b)	33. (b)	34. (a)	35. (a)	36. (c)	37. (c)	38. (a)	39. (d)	40. (b)
41. (b)	42. (b)	43. (c)	44. (c)	45. (b)	46. (b)	47. (c)	48. (a)	49. (a)	50. (c)
51. (a)	52. (c)	53. (c)	54. (c)	55. (c)	56. (c)	57. (c)	58. (b)	59. (c)	60. (c)

42. Number of circles = 7
    Number of triangles = 4
    $7 - 4 = 3$

44. Number of squares = 4

52. Ring is like a circle.

53. Number of triangles = 8
    Number of circles = 4
    Total = $8 + 4 = 12$

54. Number of squares = 6
    Number of triangles = 9
    Total = $6 + 9 = 15$

55. There is a square.

56. Hexagon has six sides.

57. Number of circles = 10

58. Shaded shape is a square.

59. Number of rectangles = $6 + 1 = 7$
    Number of circles = 10
    Total = $10 + 7 = 17$

60. Hexagon has six sides.

LOGICAL REASONING

Answer Key

1. (c)	2. (b)	3. (d)	4. (b)	5. (c)	6. (d)	7. (d)	8. (b)	9. (a)	10. (a)
11. (b)	12. (a)	13. (d)	14. (b)	15. (a)	16. (c)	17. (d)	18. (c)	19. (a)	20. (b)
21. (c)	22. (a)	23. (b)	24. (c)	25. (a)	26. (c)	27. (b)	28. (a)	29. (b)	30. (c)
31. (b)	32. (b)	33. (c)	34. (b)	35. (b)	36. (c)	37. (b)	38. (c)	39. (d)	40. (c)
41. (a)	42. (c)	43. (d)	44. (c)	45. (b)	46. (b)	47. (a)	48. (b)	49. (d)	50. (a)
51. (b)	52. (c)	53. (c)	54. (d)	55. (c)	56. (c)	57. (b)	58. (a)	59. (d)	60. (d)
61. (a)	62. (c)	63. (b)	64. (c)	65. (a)	66. (d)	67. (c)	68. (b)	69. (b)	70. (c)
71. (c)	72. (b)	73. (c)	74. (b)	75. (d)	76. (d)	77. (a)	78. (b)	79. (a)	80. (b)
81. (b)	82. (a)	83. (c)	84. (b)	85. (a)	86. (d)	87. (d)	88. (c)	89. (a)	90. (a)
91. (b)	92. (a)	93. (c)	94. (a)	95. (c)	96. (b)	97. (a)	98. (c)	99. (b)	100. (c)

1. $2 \xrightarrow{\times 3} 6 \xrightarrow{\times 3} 18 \xrightarrow{\times 3} 54$
2. $7 \times 6 = 42, 2 \times 8 = 16$
4. $16 \xrightarrow{-4} 12 \xrightarrow{-4} 8 \xrightarrow{-4} 4$
5. $72 \xrightarrow{\div 2} 36 \xrightarrow{\div 2} 18 \xrightarrow{\div 2} 9$
6. Series of prime numbers.

37. $11 \xrightarrow{+1} 12 \xrightarrow{+1} 13 \xrightarrow{+1} 14 \xrightarrow{+1} 15$
39. $9 \xrightarrow{+9} 18 \xrightarrow{+9} 27 \xrightarrow{+9} 36 \xrightarrow{+9} 45 \xrightarrow{+9} 54$
40. $56 \xrightarrow{\div 2} 28 \xrightarrow{\div 2} 14 \xrightarrow{\div 2} 7$
42. $11 \xrightarrow{-2} 9 \xrightarrow{-2} 7 \xrightarrow{-2} 5 \xrightarrow{-2} 3 \xrightarrow{-2} 1$
43. Series of prime numbers
48.

L,	O,	G,	T,	B,	Y
↓	↓	↓	↓	↓	↓
12th from start	12th from last	7th from start	7th from last	2nd from start	2nd from last

49. $A \xrightarrow{+2} C \xrightarrow{+2} E \xrightarrow{+2} G \xrightarrow{+2} I$

52. $I \xrightarrow{-3} F \xrightarrow{-3} C \xrightarrow{-3} Z \xrightarrow{-3} W \xrightarrow{-3} T$

53. A is a vowel.

54. 23 is a prime number.

56. Bangladesh is a country.

62. $16 \xrightarrow{\times 5} 80, 18 \xrightarrow{\times 5} 90$

71. $418 \xrightarrow{+4} 422 \xrightarrow{+4} 426 \xrightarrow{+4} 430$

ACHIEVERS SECTION

Answer Key

1. (c)	2. (c)	3. (b)	4. (d)	5. (a)	6. (b)	7. (c)	8. (b)	9. (c)	10. (c)
11. (a)	12. (b)	13. (b)	14. (c)	15. (d)	16. (c)	17. (a)	18. (c)	19. (d)	20. (d)
21. (a)	22. (d)	23. (b)	24. (b)	25. (a)	26. (b)	27. (b)	28. (c)	29. (b)	30. (a)
31. (c)	32. (a)	33. (b)	34. (a)	35. (c)	36. (c)	37. (b)	38. (a)	39. (b)	40. (d)

1. There are 90 2–digit numbers.
3. Largest 2–digit number = 99, smallest one digit number = 1

   ∴ Difference = 99 – 1 = 98
5. 28, 29, 30, 31, 32, 33, 34, 35, 36 → 9 numbers.
7. 1 tens = 10, 5 tens = 50, 2 ones = 2

   ∴ Sum = 10 + 50 + 2

   = 62
8. Shyam has 21 chocolates

   ∴ Ravi has (21 + 4) = 25 chocolates

   ∴ Total chocolates = 21 + 25 = 46
10. 11 tens = 110, 2 ones = 2

    ⇒ 11 tens + 2 ones = 110 + 2 = 112

    12 tens – 2 ones = 120 – 2 = 118

    11 tens – 8 ones = 110 – 8 = 102

    10 tens + 6 ones = 100 + 6 = 106

    ∴ Option (c), i.e, 102 is the least.
11. 10 Persons have 40 mangoes

    1 person has 4 mangoes.

    ∴ 5 persons have (4 + 4 + 4 + 4 + 4) = 20 mangoes.
12. Weight on left side = 15 kg

    Weight of balls on right side = 10 kg

    ∴ Weight of Ram = 15 kg – 10 kg = 5 kg
17. April, June, September and November have 30 days.
18. □ – ○ = 25 – 11 = 14
21. In 1 day, there are 24 hours.

    ∴ In 2 days, there are (24 + 24) = 48 hours.

    ∴ In 50 hours, there are 2 complete days, with 2 extra hours.

23. Date ⇒ 1 ⇒ Sunday

Date ⇒ 1 + 7 = 8 ⇒ Sunday

Date ⇒ 8 + 7 = 15 ⇒ Sunday

Date ⇒ 15 + 7 = 22 ⇒ Sunday

Date ⇒ 22 + 7 = 29 ⇒ Sunday

∴ 30th will be next day of Sunday, i.e, Monday.

24. Number of days in 1 week = 7

∴ Number of days in 3 weeks

= 7 + 7 + 7

= 21

25. The February of a leap year has 29 days.

Day on 29th ⇒ Monday

Day of (29 – 7)th; 22th ⇒ Monday

Day on (22 – 7)th; 15th ⇒ Monday

Day on (15 – 7)th; 8th ⇒ Monday

∴ Day on (8 – 7); 1st February ⇒ Monday.

27. The total money Rahim has:

= 4 × 50 + 2 × 10

= ₹ 200 + ₹ 20

= ₹ 220

28. From (23 + 17), if 23 is subtracted, the result will be 17.

∴ Required number = 23 + 17 = 40

31. 23 – 4 = 19

37. Number of boxes of sweets

= Number of times 2 can be subtracted from 18

= 9

39. Number of people in queue

= Position from right + position from left – 1

= 3 + 8 – 1

= 10

40. At start, Mohan has 2 × 100 = ₹ 200

After expenditure,

Money left = ₹ 200 – ₹ 40 = ₹ 160

Printed by Libri Plureos GmbH in Hamburg,
Germany